KHOMEINI, ISLAMIC FUNDAMENTALISM
AND THE WARRIORS OF GOD:
An Islamic Reader

A. J. Abraham

KHOMEINI, ISLAMIC FUNDAMENTALISM
AND THE WARRIORS OF GOD:
An Islamic Reader

Rhodes-Fulbright Library

by A. J. Abraham

The Rhodes-Fulbright Library

Library of Congress Catalog Card Number

99-75873

International Standard Book Number

1-55605-293-6

ProdCode: css/250/3.45/485/20

Printed in the United States of America

Wyndham Hall Press
Bristol, IN   46507-9460

DEDICATION

In memory of my co-author and friend
George I. Haddad

TABLE OF CONTENTS

PREFACE TO THE SECOND EDITION

Since the original publication of the two works that comprise this edition, popular interest in the phenomenon of Islamic Fundamentalism, as measured by the time and space of media coverage and the number of scholarly books and articles published on the subject, has continued to grow in intensity.

The emergence of Islamic Fundamentalism, sometimes called the Islamic Tendency, as depicted in our media-intensive culture, has attracted a great deal of negative attention; hardly a day passes without reports of spectacularly violent acts led by Islamic Fundamentalists. It has been said that almost one-half of all insurrections and revolts in the non-western world (the Third World) are sponsored by Islamic Fundamentalist groups and forces seeking to overthrow existing non-Moslem authorities, or Moslem governments that have failed to apply *only* Islamic Law (the Shari'ah).

The Islamic Fundamentalist groups are too numerous for a full listing, but they include: the Islamic Salvation Front in Algeria; the Moslem Brotherhood in Egypt; Hizb Allah (Hizbollah) in Lebanon; the Kosovo Liberation Army in the Balkans; the Chechen rebels in the Caucasus; the Taliban in Afghanistan; the anti-independence rebels in East Timor; the Moro Liberation Front in the Philippines; Hamas in Palestine; and the Sudanese government which is currently selling captured Animists and Christians as slaves. All these groups or movements hold a similar Islamic ideology and outlook, but that is only one Islamic point of view.

This two part compendium is based upon two studies, a book entitled: THE WARRIORS OF GOD: Jihad (Holy War) and the FUNDAMENTALISTS OF ISLAM (1989), and a monograph entitled: KHOUMANI & ISLAMIC FUNDAMENTALISM(1981); they are a modest attempt at explaining the rise of Islamic Fundamentalism from its own sources as well as an alternative to it, from the Moslem past. Therefore, the purpose of combining these two studies is to present balanced yet opposing points of view on the controversial subject of Islamic Fundamentalism, and to evoke and invite critical thinking on this complex phenomenon. This study is also designed to promote a sympathetic understanding of Islamic Fundamentalism.

A. J. Abraham
John Jay College (CUNY)

PREFACE TO PART ONE

The western view of Islamic fundamentalism, as depicted in its media, portrays that multifaceted movement sweeping across the lands of Islam as a deeply emotional and protracted struggle against western culture and thought, by a small, highly articulate, extremely volatile, and intensely vicious group of religious "fanatics."

News of their activities[1] has captured the imagination of the western press on an almost daily basis, confounding the image of Islam in the non-Moslem world. As scholars of Islam in the West, we believe that the actions depicted in the western media are only one manifestation of Islam, and although they are justified under Islamic law (the Shari'ah) as actions against violations of Islamic beliefs, they are not the only "legitimate" attitude of Islam towards non-Moslems or heterodox Moslem sects.

The former Soviet Union also viewed Islamic fundamentalism in a negative way. In its editorials, the Soviet press agency, *Tass*, criticized the movement for being a new wave of "religious repression," similar to fascism, replacing the idea of a superior race with the idea of a superior religion which oppresses other religions or "free thinkers" whose followers are assigned less civil and human rights.

Since Islam, as understood by the Marxists (Communists) opposes atheism, polytheism, panteheism, and agnostic ideologies,[2] the Soviet Union was quite naturally opposed to Islamic fundamentalism but it curbed its view, or concealed its true hostility, not to offend its large Moslem population, and in return for a degree of international co-operation from the Arab World and Moslem states at the United Nations and in international circles. (In March of 1978, the Soviet Union supported the Arab states in opposing the admission of the Arab Organization for Human Rights to consultation status in the United Nations' Economic and Social Council, for fear that the group's reports would constitute interference in the application of Islamic law towards non-Moslems and women. Under Islamic law, a woman's legal testimony is given half the weight of the legal testimony of a man, regardless of the truth of the statements presented. And, of equal importance, the Arab states have never ratified the international human rights convention because the convention's view is that secular human rights conflict with the Islamic concept of divinely ordained human rights, as derived from the Quran, Islam's Holy Scripture.)

The expanse and depth of the Islamic fundamentalist movement actually shows it to be a "reforming wave" which suggests a "revolution in reverse," and one which is without boundaries or borders. This revolution has spawned "Islamic terrorism" in the West, but those actions are seen by Moslem fundamentalists as part of a moral and ethical struggle (a jihad) against their alleged enemies or oppressors who would force the Moslems to live with cultural and legal secularism. As recently stated by Secretary-General Dr. Abd Allah Naseif of the Moslem World League in Mecca, Saudi Arabia:

> Jihad in Islam was instituted to further the cause of justice, dignity and Quranic Law through the declaration of war against forces bent on undermining these values and rights.

Thus, Dr. Naseif clearly distinguishes the differences between an offensive/defensive jihad and what the West calls "Islamic terrorism" on moral and ethical grounds rooted in the Islamic faith and in Islamic laws. The activities of Islamic fundamentalists as seen in the Moslem World, are just actions to spread the faith of Islam, to promote Islamic rights, laws, and culture, or to preserve them, undertaken by "Holy Warriors" or "Islamic Crusaders."

And, unlike the terrorism of the West undertaken by groups such as the Baader-Meinhof Gang, the Italian Red Brigades, or the Japanese Red Army whose objectives, methods and rationale are completely secular, the actions undertaken by Islamic fundamentalists are always Islamic in their objectives, methods and rationale. There is nothing un-Islamic about "Islamic terrorism" or "Holy War," the common misnomers for jihad.

It is, therefore, essential and proper to understand the phenomenon of Islamic fundamentalism and the precepts of jihad in order to form a more positive view, policy, and response to it from the West.

The nucleus of this study will examen the ethical and moral aspects of jihad (Islamic struggle) which is one of the "twin pillars" of Islamic fundamentalism. The other pillar, Islamic law–which sanctions jihad–has been examined elsewhere,[3] particularly the legal aspect of jihad which we shall briefly touch upon.

Islamic fundamentalism has commanded a great deal of attention on a world-wide basis, particularly in regard to the tragic situation in Lebanon. Because of its importance for that region of our world and the superpowers as well Islamic fundamentalism deserves our fair and serious attention.

The tone of this study is sympathetic and explanatory and, hopefully, it will lead to a better understanding of Islam, jihad, and the generally frightening phenomenon of "Islamic terrorism."

I am, indeed, indebted to numerous Islamic organizations for suggesting, supporting and commenting upon this study, particularly Islam and the West, International Cultural Association, The Islamic Foundation, The Islamic Council of Europe, and several members of the Islamic Foreign Minister's Conference (1986).

And now, a brief personal note. The bulk of this study on the doctrine of jihad was originally presented by my co-author, Rev. Dr. George I. Haddad, as a thesis at Princeton Theological Seminary under the title: *The Doctrine of Jihad in Islam.*

Dr. Haddad's untimely death in October of 1985 cut short a brilliant career dedicated to the advancement of human rights, the spirit of toleration, love, and ecumenism in Christian-Moslem relations, as well as among Christian sects. The passing of my friend, mentor, and co-author has left a void that can not be filled. Those of us who knew Dr. Haddad will miss his comradery, scholarship, and personal traits of decency, generosity, integrity, as well as his unbounded humanity.

Lastly, I wish to express my greatful appreciation to Mr. John A. Cardello for editing this manuscript.

A. J. Abraham

NOTES

1. For the activities of the Islamic fundamentalist see: A. J. Abraham, "The Theory and Practice of Islamic Fundamentalists," in *Transnational Perspectives*, vol. 11, no. 4, 1985, p. 20.

2. A. J. Abraham, *Islam and Christianity: Crossroads in Faith*, IN.: Wyndham Hall Press, 1987, 46-47.

3. Still the best legal study of jihad can be found in: Majid Khadduri, *War and Peace in the Law of Islam*, Baltimore: Johns Hopkins Press, 1955, also see: Majid Khadduri and Herbert J. Liebesny, *Law in the Middle East*, vol. 1, Wash.: The Middle East Institute, 1955, pp. 353-360; Anwar Ahmed Qadri, *Islamic Jurisprudence in the Modern World*, Lahore: Ashraf Pub. House, 1981, pp. 282-283; Muhammad Hamidullah, *The Muslim Conduct of State*, Lahore: Ashraf Pub. House, 1977.

PART ONE

THE WARRIORS OF GOD:
Jihad (Holy War) and the
Fundamentalists of Islam

A. J. Abraham
George I. Haddad
New York Institute of Technology

It is He Who hath sent
His Apostle with Guidance
And the Religion of Truth
To proclaim it
Over all religions...

(Q 9:33)

INTRODUCTION

To a considerable extent, all Moslems are fundamentalists, that is, they believe that the Quran (Koran), the Holy Scripture of Islam, is God's (Allah's) final, complete, and perfected revelation for all mankind. The Quran is, therefore, the supreme guide for the human race, the direct words of God, covering all aspects of human life, transmitted directly to His last prophet and messenger, Muhammad. Its priority supersedes all other Scriptures, past, present and future on all matters of human existence.

Next in importance for Moslems is the discourse of the Prophet Muhammad as recorded in the collections of his speech (the Hadith), followed by the prophet's customary behavior, called the Sunnah (actually purified Arabian culture).

The Quran, the Hadith, and the Sunnah form a Moslem's primary cultural identity and basic patterns of thought. Centuries ago, these three sources helped to foment the great conquests of Islam, the Islamic state, and the Islamic legal system (the Shari'ah/the path).

Islam is God's plan for the world,[1] every inch of it, not just the Islamic regions. Islam is for everyone, whether one wants it or not. It is the duty of every Moslem to help expand the borders of Islam until every being on this planet acknowledges that "There is no God but Allah and Muhammad is His Messenger."

Islam is a missionary religion, and an ever expanding faith. It rejects the validity of all other ideologies and belief-systems, religious or secular, with only Jews, Christians, and Sabians protected from forced conversion as People of The Book (Ahl al-Kitab) or as People of a Covenant (Ahl al-Dhimma), who possess a legitimate yet, nevertheless, falsified revelation.

With these facts in mind, we can now define the Islamic fundamentalist movement from their own constructs. Western scholars, analyzing this phenomenon, have used modern political terms to express its dimensions. Terms[2] such as "militant Islam," "Islamic resurgence," or "Islamic revival" (or revivalism), or Islamic fundamentalism have appeared in books, articles, and in the media. These terms, however, do not exactly fit the phenomenon, but for lack of a more exact term in western languages, "Islamic fundamentalism" is probably the best to use. The other terms, "militant Islam" explains little other than the violence ("Islamic terrorism") associated with the movement; while "resurgence" or "revival" suggests the notion of a cyclical or semi-dormant activity, that comes and goes, rather than an always present,[3] growing, churning undercurrent.

A Moslem fundamentalist, however, would probably reject the use of all those terms and refer to himself as a struggler (a jihadi/mujahid) in the path of God (fi sabel Allah). Although physically in our present day and age, from a psychological perspective, the Islamic fundamentalist sees himself as a sixth century companion of the Prophet Muhammad fighting the enemies of God. In his mind, heart and soul, he is a timeless warrior, other-world oriented, battling the evils that men do. He is a stoic fatalist on a holy mission in a Satanic world that he wishes to purify.

Since all Moslems share the same fundamental beliefs, what then truly distinguishes the passive Moslem at peace with himself and the world from the active Moslem who has embarked upon a violent struggle (the jihadi)? The answer lies in the interpretation of Quranic verses. The passive Moslem fundamentalist believes that Islam will encompass the world by peaceful, evolutionary, means because God has willed it. The active Moslem fundamentalist believes that Islam will conquer the world by militaristic, revolutionary means specifically because God has ordained fighting ("killing") in His cause for the believer (Q 2:216). And, the passivist tries to fit Islam into the existing world order, whereas the activist wants to fit the world into Islamic culture. And, finally, the controversy may be traced back to the origins of the word Islam itself. Its tri-litteral root forms the words for peace and for submission. The passivist views Islam as a religion of peace; the activist sees the establishment of peace on Earth only after all people have submitted to Islam and its laws, by force if necessary.

The activist or militant fundamentalist criticizes the passive or moderate fundamentalist for having lost "the spirit of jihad," by becoming too friendly, too soft towards the non-Moslems (beings or states), contrary to Quranic injunctions (Q 5:54).

Furthermore, the activist believes that he can not lose, because Islam can not be defeated. Should he succeed in his earthly mission or endeavors, he is seen as a hero by the like-minded; should he die in the process, he is seen as a martyr (a shahid) who has gone directly to paradise. In either case, he is a fearless winner and, in his mind, a person to be idolized. He has obtained ideological immortality among the faithful.

As far as the activist (jihadi/militant) fundamentalist, hearafter referred to as Islamic fundamentalist, is concerned, the world is divided into two hostile spheres,[4] dar al-Islam (the abode of peace/surrender) and dar al-harb (the abode of war). All wars in Islam must be religious in intent, to open new lands to the faith and to covert their inhabitants, or to defend the lands of Islam from foreign forces or ideas (ideological pollution). This relationship must endure until the entire world is totally Islamified. The fundamentalists tell their followers that the non-Moslem World is their enemy, and that only a temporary truce with them is permissible. Consequently, Islam may wage war against otherwise friendly states because they are not guided by Islamic principles and laws.

Western scholars, "intoxicated by the image of Saladin," as well as some Moslem intellectuals influenced by western scholarship, have portrayed the spread of Islam as a peaceful venture, the results of missionaries preaching the truth. Long gone are the pre-World War II depictions of Islam as a "bloody" and "militant" religion "spread by the sword." However, the Islamic fundamentalist does not concur with that view at all!

The Prophet Muhammad went on the offensive against the enemies of God from the city of Medinah. He won three major victories over the Meccans at Badr, at Uhud, and during the seige of Medinah.[5] Within a hundred years of the prophet's death in 632 A.D., the Arab armies had defeated both the Byzantine forces in the Near East, and the Persian Empire as well. They fought several campaigns to conquer North Africa and faced rough going in Central Asia, until permanent conquest and occupation was achieved. In sub-Saharan Africa, violent jihads continued well into the nineteenth century, destroying the indigenous African culture. Only in south-east Asia, conversion by peaceful means has been recorded, but doubt has been shed upon that tradition[6] as well. (Some Moslem scholars believe that without jihad in its violent, war-like urge, Islam might have remained the local religion of an Arabian clan or tribe (Q 42:7).

All Islamic fundamentalists believe that God has sanctioned fighting for them because they are fighting for God's truth and to bring the blessings of Islam to all mankind. Once military victory over the non-Moslem is achieved, then an Islamic state can be created and Islamic law, the most peaceful tool in the arsenal for conversion, can be imposed to bring about the total Islamification of the nation, by setting the standard for what is permissible and what is not.[7]

There are several easily discernible factors that have undercut the efforts of moderate, passive, Moslems and, thereby, fostered and sustained the rise and prominence of Islamic fundamentalism.

These factors include:

1.   The Arab-Israeli conflict–this conflict is seen by the fundamentalists as a western intrusion into dar al-Islam resulting in the transformation of Palestine into a Jewish and Zionist state–has deeply affected the fundamentalist view, as a new form of neo-colonization[8] or a Crusade for Jerusalem.

2.   The legacy of European colonization in the post World War I period created feelings of inferiority or damaged esteem (self-respect) or hurt pride, among devout Moslems. Something has gone wrong in the scheme of things, in God's plan for the world, putting the non-Moslems in a position of power over the Moslems.[9]

3.   Neo-colonization in the post World War II period caught the newly independent Arab and Moslem states between the rivalries of the bi-polar superpowers, the United States and the Soviet Union. Nominally independent, those states found themsleves economically and technologically dependent upon the foreign powers which the fundamenalists believe have more in common (their secular life styles) than not, thus outweighing "the differences between them."[10] This is best expressed in the slogan: "Neither East nor West, Islam is the best."

4.   The Soviet Union, in particular, faced an additional, ideological, problem being an officially atheistic state based upon the thoughts and teachings of Karl Marx and V. I. Lenin. In fundamentalist eyes, this made the Soviet Union an eternal and implacable enemy of God. As such, the fundamentalists of Islam are in a constant state of jihad against them. Its culture is, therefore, anathema to Moslems world-wide.

5.   The rabid anti Americanism of the Moslem fundamentalists results from an equally hostile understanding of American culture. American culture has had a profound impact upon the non-western world in recent times; it is rapidly affecting the way of life of the world's youth, certainly those who are less traditional than their parents. America's human rights campaigns, the quest for world-wide racial, ethnic, religious, and sexual equality and justice has impacted negatively upon the Islamic fundamentalists, for they believe that a persons rights and the roles they are allowed to play or are assigned in life are divinely ordained and established in the Quran, for all mankind.[11] The intrusion of western ideas or values defies Islamic culture and law[12] and has affected the public and private lives of many by "assimilation or adoption or domination," all of which are alien to the Islamic tradition, producing a huge culture conflict between Islam and the West.

Islam has been negatively criticized in the West for going against the historical trend of total equality for all people and, to date, no Moslem clergyman has spoken out in support of equal rights for non-Moslems, Moslem religious minorities, or women, in the World of Islam. But, it must be stated in defense of Islam that many western scholars are unaware of Islam's "spiritual," non-political, non-legal, "equality," based upon the our common descent from Adam.

(Unlike Islam, Christianity exhorts absolute equality in regard to race, religion, and sex, as a teaching of Christ. Eloquently put forth in St. Paul's letter to the Galatians, Christianity teaches that:

There is neither jew nor Greek,
there is neither slave nor free,
there is neither male nor female,
for you are all one,
in union with Jesus Christ...

Thus, the Christian West developed a different view of human rights. When it failed to live up to its own standards, it failed because of human folly, not because of a religious precept.)

In Islam there are rigorously defined levels for all mankind. Equality for Moslem men exists, followed by Moslem women, veiled and protected from the temptations of Moslem men, and to prevent them from becomoing westernized "sex objects;" then come the Christians and Jews (the dhimmis) and, lastly are the pagans.

The often quoted Quranic verses in defense of Islamic rights bears repetition here:

> Then when the sacred months have
> passed, slay the idolaters where-
> ever ye find them, and take
> them captive, and besiege them...   (Q 9:5)

> Fight those who believe not...nor
> acknowledge the religion of
> truth (Islam) of the people
> of the book
> (Jews/Christians/Sabians)
> until they pay Jizya
> (A tax or fine)
> And feel themselves subdued.
> (Lowly/humiliated/persecuted)   (Q 9:29)

> Fighting is prescribed
> for you, and ye dislike it.
> But it is possible
> that ye dislike a thing
> Which is good for you,
> And that ye love a thing
> Which is bad for you.
> But God knoweth,
> And ye know not.   (Q 2:216)

Regarding the rights of women, the Quran says:

> Your women are a tilth (a field)
> to you (to cultivate) so go to
> your tilth as ye will,
> But do some good act
> for your souls beforehand...   (Q 2:223)

and

>Men are in charge of women
>because God hath made the one
>to excell (be superior over) the
>other, and because they spend of their
>property (for the support or maintenance
>of women)...
>As for those from whom ye fear rebellion,
>admonish them and banish them to beds apart,
>and scourge them (beat them).
>But if they return to obedience (to you),
>Seek not against them
>means (of annoyance/forgive them)
>For God is Most High,
>Great (above you all)   (Q 4:34)

"Islam put one half of the human race, women, into a position subordinate to the male half–no amount of apologetics about respect for women, protection of their just rights and so forth can get around this basic and unjust discrimination,"[13] and, furthermore, Islamic law assigns half value to a woman's legal testimony.

A Moslem modernist's response to the belief that Islam discriminates against women would be to say that Islam simply favors men (reverse discrimination?), while protecting women from becoming sex objects. In Islam, it is said: "Women are obliged to provide sexual satisfaction to their husbands, but they may refuse all else." Practically, however, they are subject to the will of men who see them as "sexual receptacles."

In the Moslem fundamentalist view, the western world is seen in a "pornographic" light.[14] Consequently, they oppose western "customs relating to sex, female athletics, co-education, employment, mixed social life, and mixed swimming, dancing, dating, attendance at night clubs, and so on,"[15] all of which they believe contribute to female immorality, loss of virginity, illegitimate births, and worst of all, the establishment of equal rights for women and control over their own bodies.

Clearly, Islam's traditional society and modern western society hold very different attitudes on women and, therefore, they have evolved differently on similar but basic issues of human rights.

In all fairness to Islamic culture regarding women, some Islamic fundamentalists maintain that the veiling of women may be a necessary evil but, in fact, it enables Moslem women to circulate freely among Moslem men, free from the fear of molestation. They believe that the separation of men and women, outside of immediate family relations, has made Moslem men "overheated" or "sexually hypertense" in search for "sexual receptacles," and that an "exposed" woman might trigger a males' unwanted sexual advances or responses, possibly endangering the women' life. The veil, therefore, protects Moslem girls and women, in regard to Islamic attitudes towards the female. Moslem women in a western society do not need that added protection when outside a Moslem neighborhood, but it is still recommended in areas with a large Moslem concentration. Non-Moslem women should also dress accordingly when they are in an Islamic atmosphere, for safety sake, although the rationale for it remains largely incomprehensible to them. The use of the veil by women in the world of Islam makes them feel protected.

The fundamentalists believe that human rights are immutable and that the 'words of god" supercede the "constructs of man." There are, consequently, specific levels of humanity (tabaqat al-insaniyah) for all mankind in Islam, based primarily on one's faith and gender.

> 6.   Most contemptuous in the Moslem fundamentalist's eye is secularism, in idea or institution, as we understand it in the West.[16] As seen by them it is a meaningless concept at best, or an enemy of God at worst. This view covers all aspects or modes of life; cultural (art, music, literature), social, sexual, political, economic, and even mental; this perspective includes, of course, law and education as well. The fundamentalists see secular values as attempts to "pollute" pure Islam by rejecting Islam's moral and ethical principles in order to oppress the Moslem masses, but the Moslems will reject secularism when the plot is discovered, because the words of God will always have more appeal to them than any secular ideology.[17]

The current Moslem governments, whether kingdoms or republics, can neither avoid nor appease the all searching, all inclusive, eye of the fundamentalists. The most devout are the most devoutly opposed to their own governments, but some seek to win political power through existing norms while others seek to overthrow their governments and replace them with a purely revolutionary one.[18] They all maintain, in one way or another, that the current governments in the Moslem World have become the "stooges" of the superpowers[19] on the international level, and have departed from Islamic values and laws at home.[20] In some countries the fundamentalists have formed "shadow governments" including their own schools, clinics and self-help projects and institutions, and they have obtained extensive financial contributions from the rich and the poor.

The official governments watch the fundamentalists but they can not effectively oppose them because they justify their actions and statements in Quranic terms; in quotes from the Quran, in reference to the Prophet Muhammad, and in Islamic symbolism. They expand their activities through a network of mosques and beyond by establishing cells that utilize tape recordings of key sermons. No government can oppose the fundamentalists without seeming to oppose Islam or to quiet them unless they commit a criminal act, and then, they cite religion in their defense to intimidate the judicial process. Meanwhile, the liberal scholars and politicians constantly come under attack for deviating from their faith, and have little support, so that they continue to lose ground to the radicals.[21]

Furthermore, the existing governments can not create alternate ideologies for the youth to believe in such as "nationalism, rationalism, popular sovereignty, secularism, liberalism, western law codes and education, humanism, or materialism," for the fundamentalists claim that there is no place for those ideas in an Islamic state or entity.[22] Thus, the government sits alone at the top. The experiments with Arab Socialism in Nassarist Egypt, or the Shah's White Revolution in Iran, even when disguised as Islamic Socialism failed to resolve existing problems,[23] because it was seen as foreign, an attempt to "compromise" Islam or force it to "co-exist" with something un-Islamic, and consequently those efforts were undermined from the start.

Grafting a modern superstructure upon a traditional cultural base can never succeed. Thorough-going reforms require support from the clergy and a total commitment to modern education and values. If reforms are not carried out in depth in traditional societies, then they are truly destined to fail.

The Islamic fundamentalist movement is not as monolithic as it may appear to the outside world. Although all fundamentalists share common views, the movement varies in context and in methodology from one country to the next, and among different sects and groups within a nation. Membership also varies from place to place with floaters entering and leaving a hard core cell, formed about a charismatic leader, usually the shaykh (religious leader) of a mosque. Those religious leaders who form the ulema (clergy) maintain their independence from the central government and are often beyond the reach of the state. This has been the pattern of organization from the time of Ibn Taymiyah (d. 1328), Muhammad abd al-Wahhab (d. 1792), Jamal al-Din al-Afghani (d. 1897) to current leaders such as: Sayyid Qubt, (1906-1966), Mawlanna Abu al-Ala Mawdudi (1903-1979), Shaykh Sa'id Sha'ban, Imam Musa al-Sadr, Shaykh Husayn Fadl Allah, Muhammad Mehdi Shams al-Din, Subhi al-Tufayli, and of course, the Ayatollah Khomeini,[24] all of whom expound similar themes.

They recruit volunteers from all walks of life, from the illiterate to the most literate, from the urban and rural poor to the prominent and wealthy. But it is the young educated Moslems who lead and fuel the movement. Often frustrated by personal or national failures; seeing themselves or their states on the back-shelf of civilization; dwelling upon past glory days when Islam was on the march, they have become angry young men who have turned to faith for revenge against their perceived enemies in the hope of regaining lost prestige. Simply and eloquently put by Shaykh Hassan al-Banna, founder of the Moslem Brotherhood:

> It is in the nature of Islam to dominate, not to be dominated, to impose its law on all nations and to extend its power to the entire planet.

Those young men control the schools and universities through student groups; they are generally science and engineering majors, law and medical students, and a few from those who seek education in the liberal, humanistic arts. They can be seen roaming the campuses harassing non-Moslems or "throwing acid on the face and bodies of women who are not dressed in Islamic costume." Others can be found in the military and, in fact, in all professions and occupations.

The common beliefs of all Islamic fundamentalists, young or old, relate to well established Islamic norms, as interpreted by the Islamic clergy. For the fundamentalist, Islam is everything, and the only thing of any importance. All else is either meaningless or superfluous, at best. Gleaning the works of Moslem fundamentalists, past and present, yields some common ideological perspectives.

In the simple phrase: "Islam is," (Islam exists), the fundamental truth of Islam is expressed. Islam has arrived for all mankind, God's greatest gift to His creatures. Every Moslem understands and believes that. Clearly for the non-Moslem, "Islam is the religion of the Moslem; to the Moslem, Islam is the religion of God"[25] and, consequently, Islamic culture is the "culture of God," for all humanity.

The will of God is embodied in both the collective will of the Islamic community (the ummah) and in the spirit of jihad in the individual; to implement God's divinely ordained culture is the main objective of the Islamic mission.[26] That mission today is exactly the same as the commission given by God to Muhammad to cleanse the ka'bah (the pre-Islamic shrine) of paganism. Islam came into existence to replace all other religions and ideologies. Thus, it became the source of Arabian culture, and basic Islamic culture was reproduced everywhere the Arabian conquerors went, on both the private and public levels.[27] As Islam spread throughout the eastern world, it developed a "dynamic creativity in history,"[28] but remained a closed system, neither open to additions nor subtractions from the understood Quranic text or ideal: the Sunnah or the Hadith. The Book of Guidance (the Quran) is the centepiece of the Islamic faith, and it continues to shape Islam's past, present and future.[29]

Thus, Islam became a world-wide culture, on its way to becoming God's plan for the world. It is perfect, as such, because it is God's vision of what He wants for us. It must be applied as revealed without deformity; Islam is the "final arbiter of all that is..."[30] and it must be applied universally, as it existed in the seventh century,[31] in accordance with the Prophet's saying:

> The best generation is my generation, then the ones who follow, and then those who follow them.

The idea of progress in Islam[32] is not rooted in material well-being, in human rights, or in social or cultural advances. It is rooted in the attempt to recreate the prophet's time, to create the Islamic classical ideal. It lies in going "back to the future," towards the best generation, the best of times, when the Prophet Muhammad walked and talked among us. Cultural development, as understood in the West, is "a dead concept," in Islam. It has no place in an Islamic state and, thus, the Islamic state has no need for it.

Can this objective be achieved or is it just "wishful thinking about days gone by"? The fundamentalists of Islam believe that they can achieve their objectives and, furthermore, they are in agreement on how and where to proceed.

The first place to start is at home. Just as the Prophet Muhammad purged the Ka'bah in Mecca before the great Islamic conquest, the fundamentalists must purge their own societies of all non-Islamic concepts or institutions. This is called the search for "authenticity" as expressed in the Arabic words: asala (basics/origins), islah (reform), tajdid (renewal), and nahda (uplifting/renaissance).[33] The main thrust of all this is to "rediscover or re-become ourselves." The first step is to eliminate foreign intrusions in the Moslem World, those innovations (bid'ah) are the product of foreign cultures, governments, and institutions imposed upon Islam by its corrupt, westernized, political leadership. Hence, the fundamentalists are against their own state; they encourage their followers to disregard their govern-ments, and actively oppose it, if possible, in order to create an Islamic state, a modern theocracy of sorts and a world as God has ordained it.

There is no clear, concise, description or policy regarding the exact nature of the Islamic state that will replace existing kingdoms, dictatorships, or republics. The topic is still much in debate, although that objective is agreed upon by all of the fundamentalists.[34] The Islamic state must not be subject to the affairs of non-Moslems,[35] nor make alliances with non-Moslem states, even if there is a commonality of goals,[36] because the Islamic state is a devine entity, its "God's state or His kingdom" on Earth.[37] It does not need nor want any partners!

It, therefore, follows that at the head of the Islamic state is God, followed by the Prophet Muhammad who received the Quran. The Holy Scripture of Islam has both religious and administrative chapters (suras) which call for the Islamic state (ummah/community) which can never err. Once the state exists, it applies Islamic law at home and conducts warfare (jihad) abroad.

The Islamic state may be led by either a clergyman or layman, but never by a women or a member of a religious minority.[38] In an Islamic state, Islam is the ideology of the state and, therefore, there is no room for those who are outside the state's ideology in the government; they are seen as third-class citizens or aliens and, possibly, dangerous creatures whose loyalty is questioned and always suspect. Allegiance belongs to God, and a Moslem, in or out of an Islamic state, owes no allegiance to anyone but God, and obedience to His duly ordained representatives and laws. Moslems living as citizens of non-Moslem countries should not take their allegiance to those states seriously, for that could place them in serious jeopardy when war resumes between those states and Islam. Citizenship must never obstruct the spread of Islam. (Recently, in the West, Moslem citizens in Europe and America have been exempt from pledges of allegiance and military service, on conscientious objector gounds).

The most important aspect of an Islamic state is the acceptance and application of *only* Islamic law; Islamic law is essential to the legitmacy of the state and its leadership; it is the criteria to measure the Islamicness of the entity.[39]

The law establishes the norms for society; it is prescriptive and, therefore, leads the society into conformity.[40] It places religious minorities and women in their proper place; and it prevents a secular state from emerging or surviving in a non-secular society.

The importance of the law is all consuming because it is God who rules through it, and anyone who adds secular law to the state refutes or opposes the will of God, and acts arrogantly towards Him.[41] Moslem individuals or Islamic societies can not, should not accept secular law or the laws of other religions because that is blasphemous.[42]

The combination of an Islamic state under Islamic law, with all the foreign contradictions removed, is a powerful entity, capable of initiating conquest in the path of God. It would have the legitimacy and approval of God. It could face the future with a success oriented policy to resolve all the problems it faces, and liberate all mankind.

Islam solves all problems, the fundamentalists believe. The application of Islam and its laws, in their minutest details, will resolve all present and future problems, so that nothing else is needed. The fundamentalist approach is based on the assumption that "the problems contemporary Arab society is facing are not new, and that the past offers a solution for them."[43] This may seem naive to some, but Islam's objective is to transform the world back to the Prophet Muhammad's time when modern problems did not exist, and to use the concept of *maslaha* (correcting) as a theory of legal reasoning or judgement (ijtihad).[44] Nevertheless, even in a non-evolutionary, prescriptive, culture or society new problems will emerge and Islamic justice may not be accepted by all, even if Islam becomes a mass ideology, because several new interpretations may arise.

For non-Moslems, Islamic justice remains a unique point of view that seems to act unjustly towards them, but in an Islamic state, they count for little, and are made to feel that they don't belong there. Conversion, of course, will resolve the handicap, and end all religious and political contradictions.

Next the Islamic state must deal with the "foreign" cancers imbeded in the Islamic body which has produced festering sores that irritate the fundamentalist's world view. Therefore, a great deal of attention is focused upon Israel and Lebanon.

The fundamentalists oppose Israel because it exists, and acts as a threat to them.[45] They may or may not care much about Palestinian-Israeli politics, but they all agree that Jerusalem must be liberated and remain a Moslem city, forever. It may have been holy to Jews and Christians at one time, but, today, it is holy to Islam, and that's what counts. As farr as the state of Israel is concerned, it is an affront to Islam, a persecutor of Moslem Palestinians, and an occupier of Islamic territory (dar al-Islam). Its transformation into an Islamic state is an imperative. (The most extreme fundamentalists still lament the loss of land in Europe that was once occupied by the Arabs and Turks, in centuries gone by.)

Almost as negative as Israel in the fundamentalist view is Lebanon, not because it has caused any harm to Islam or to its Moslem citizens, but because it had established equality among all its various sects.[46] Lebanon is called a Christian state because its president is a Christian, but it has a large Moslem population which the fundamentalists imagine have been "victimized" or "neglected" by the state. They call the Christians the remnants of the Crusaders[47] but, obviously, that's ludicrous because the Christians are the indigenous inhabitants. (The success of the Lebanese

Christians is the product of human resource development and, certainly, not due to the exploitation of any sect at the hands of the others.)

Outside its immediate grasp but, nevertheless, a main objective of Islamic fundamentalism is the Third World which the fundamentalists want to incorporate into the Moslem World. The Third World, in the fundamentalist eye, consists of a hodgepodge of meaningless and worthless religions and customs that survive in weak and exploited states. Thus, Islam in the non-western world is advancing as a liberating force,[48] to free those unfortunate and exploited states from being trapped between the two great Satans: the United States and the former Soviet Union.

The inhabitants of the Third World, however, do not see Islam in that light, as a savior of sorts, but rather as a foreign ideology that will destroy their native cultural belief-systems. Islamic fundamentalism does not promise improved economic development, political democracy, religious freedom, or a modern social and cultural life which they desperately need there, but only spiritual equality for men after conversion. In fact, the Third World fears the Islamic fundamentalist movement precisely because they see it as a new wave or form of religious and cultural imperialism.

In defense of Islamic fundamentalism and its Third World politics, we may conclude that it has offered the non-western world an alternative to being caught between the superpowers.[49] But its ultimate objective is to eliminate the two powerful, bi-polar, camps, and end their secular ways of life; to terminate their "ungodly" activities in our world so that this planet will be ruled as God wants it, in accordance with His will as expressed in traditional Islamic culture.

We must now pose the question of how will an Islamic world come about? What is the fundamentalist plan? Is it really possible? Obviously, the Moslem extremists think it will, but they disagree on the method. This results from both historical perspectives and theological inferences.

Upon the death of the Prophet Muhammad, an election was held to select an administrative successor (caliph) to him. The Moslem community was split between those who believed that any male Moslem could rule, and those who insisted that the only candidate must be Ali, the cousin and son-in-law of the prophet. The former are called Sunnite Moslems while the latter are known as Shi'ite Moslems.

These two communities or sects drifted apart, as their relationship grew hostile. The controversy was to be settled in 680 A.D. near Karbala, in Iraq, where the Sunnite forces of Damascus under Yazid clashed with the Shi'ite troops of Ali's son, Imam Husayn. Husayn's forces and his entourage were massacred; since then the Sunnite Moslems have controlled most of the Islamic world while the Shi'ites went underground by dissimulation (taqiyah), succeeding in their efforts only in Iran.

Since the battle of Karbala, the Shi'ites have held a collective feeling of frustration and guilt for not coming to the aid of Imam Husayn; they have developed a "mind-set" on martyrdom to free themselves and their families from that overbearing guilt. And, they continue to nurture a powerful hostility towards the Sunnite establishment.

The political consequence of that event is enormous; the Shi'ites maintain that all governments are illegal pending rule by a descendent of Husayn. In the absence of the proper person, only the clergy may rule as a caretaker government, until the missing Imam (religious leader) Muhammad al-Muntazar, the Mahdi (the guide) reappears. He is currently in occultation, after disappearing in infancy and is expected to return when Karbala falls to the Shi'ites by war or insurrection. The Sunnites, in the meantime, have continually persecuted the Shi'ites, only recognizing their legitimacy in this century.

Based upon those historic and theological precedents, different theories have been advanced on the key issues of Islamic expansion.

Among the Islamic fundamentalists, the Sunnites believe that the transformation of the non-Moslem states into Islamic ones will come about by simulation of the course of events undertaken during the great Islamic conquest of the seventh century.[50] At that time, the Moslems gained a victory over the superpowers of that day, the Byzantine and Persian Empires, when those two states fought to the point of exhaustion over the Near East. Until recently, the fundamentalists believed that a clash of destinies will occur between the superpowers over the unresolvable, on-again, off-again, Arab-Israeli conflict. The United States and the Soviet Union will exhaust themselves in the conflagration, and Islam will march forward again, as in the past.

For the Shi'ite Moslems, Islamification of the non-Moslem world will occur by messianic means, upon the return of the Mahdi.[51] This will happen when the Shi'ites reverse the course of history, by fighting the battle of Karbala once again, and winning it. They are "riding a time-machine" into the past, in the belief that winning this battle will vindicate them and convince the Sunnites to adjust their creed, accept Shi'ism and join the Mahdi in a final assault upon the enemies of Islam and all who reject the true faith.

As of this writing, no one can ascertain what will happen in the Near East, but the extremists are convinced that this new "Islamic Crusade" will succeed for God has promised success to those who follow Him. This attitude is best exemplified by the declaration of Ayatollah Ruhollah Khomeini:[52]

> The governments of the world should know that Islam can not be defeated. Islam will be victorious in all the countries of the world, and Islam and the teachings of the Koran will prevail all over the world.

§ § §

NOTES

1. Q 9:33. (All Quranic quotes are taken from A. Yusuf Ali's edition entitled *THE HOLY QUR-AN*.); Abraham, *op. cit.*, p. v.

2. See: John L. Esposito., (ed.), *Voices of Resurgent Islam*, N.Y.: Oxford Univ. Press, 1983, p. 3.

3. Ziauddin Sardar, *Islamic Futures: The Shape of Things To Come*, London: Mansell Pub., 1985, p. 44.

4. Alan R. Taylor, "The Political Psychology of Islamic Resurgence In The Middle East," *American Arab Affairs*, Spring, 1983, no. 4, p. 130; Amin Taheri, *Holy Terror*, N.Y.: Adler and Adler, 1987, pp. 10, 21, 203.

5. *Ibid.*; Abraham, *op. cit.*, pp. 42-43.

6. P. M. Holt, Ann K. S. Lambton and Bernard Lewis, (ed.), *The Cambridge History of Islam*, vol. 2, Cambridge: At The Univ. Press, 1970, part vi, ch. 1, p. 123.

7. Abraham, *op. cit..*, pp. 58-60.

8. Esposito, *op. cit.*, pp. 12, 217; For a brief description of fundamentalist attitudes on Jews and Zionism by Omar Telmessani (d. 1986), leader of the Moslem Brotherhood in Egypt, see: Ronald L. Nettler, "Islam vs. Israel," *Commentary*, vol. 78, no. 6, Dec., 1984, pp. 26-30; Maridi Nahas, "State-Systems And Revolutionary Challenge: Nassar, Khomeini, and the Middle East," in *International Journal of Middle East Studies*, vol. 17, no. 4, Nov. 1985, p. 515.

9. First indicated in Wilfred Cantwell Smith's *Islam in Modern History*, N.Y.: The New American Library, 1957, p. 48; Robin Wright, *Sacred Rage, The Wrath of Militant Islam*, N.Y.: Simon and Schuster, 1986, p. 252; Marvin Zonis, "Iran: A Theory of Revolution from Accounts of The Revolution," *World Politics*, vol. Xxxv, no. 4, July 1983, p. 599.

10. Esposito, *op. cit.*, pp. 12, 215; Daniel Pipes, "Fundamentalist Moslems, Between America and Russia," *Foreign Affairs*, Summer, 1986, pp. 939-941, 955.

11. On this see: Abraham, *op. cit.*, pp. 51-54; G. H. Jensen, *Militant Islam*, N.Y.: Harper and Row, 1979, pp. 14-15.

12. Esposito, *Voices...*, pp. 12, 48, 53; J. L. Esposito, "Islam in the Politics of the Middle East," in *Current History*, Feb. 1986, p. 81; Jansen, *op. cit.*, p. 107; Nahas, *op. cit.*, p. 520; Farzeen Nasri, "Iranian Studies And The Iranian Revolution," *World Politics*, vol. Xxxv, no. 4, July 1983, p. 628; Pipes, *op. cit.*, pp. 946, 955-956; Taheri, *op. cit.*, p. 207.

13. Quoted from Jansen, *op. cit.*, pp. 210, 184-185; On Islamic slavery and race relations see: Bernard Lewis, *Race And Color in Islam*, N.Y.: Harper Torchbooks, 1971.

14. Pipes, *op. cit.*, pp. 943-944, 951.

15. *Ibid.*, p. 940.

16. Abraham, *op. cit.*, p. 58; Mahmoud H. Farghal, "Islamic Ideology: Essence and Dimensions," *American-Arab Affairs*, no. 4, Spring, 1983, pp. 100-101; M. Farhang and J. H. Motavalli, "Iran: A Great Leap Backward," in *The Progressive*, August, 1984, p. 20; *International Institute of Islamic Thought, Islamization of Knowledge: General Principles And Work Plan*, 1987, pp. vii-viii, 37-38; Jensen *op. cit.*, pp. 18, 74, 126-127; Taheri, *op. cit.*, pp. 22, 205; John O. Voll, *Islam: Continuity and Change in the Modern World*, Colorado: Westview Press, p. 282.

17. Alan R. Taylor, "The Political Psychology of Islamic Resurgence In The Middle East," *American-Arab Affairs*, no. 4 Spring, 1983, pp. 127-128; Hassan Hanifi, "The Origins of Violence in Contemporary Islam," in *Development*, no. 1, 1987, p. 58.

18. Esposito, "Islam in The Politics...," p. 54; Voll, *op. cit.*, p. 315. Also see; Emmanuel Sivan, *Radical Islam: Medieval Theology and Modern Politics*, New Haven: Yale Univ. Press, 1985. Taheri, *op. cit.*, p. 26.

19. Nahas, *op. cit.*, p. 521.

20. Pipes, *op. cit.*, pp. 944-945.

21. Nasri, *op, cit.*, pp. 608-609; Wright, *op. cit.*, p. 61.

22. Esposito, *Voices...*, p. 7; Jansen, *op. cit.*, pp. 126-127. For the opposite point of view, the compatibility of Islam with democracy, socialism and secular law see; A. J. Abraham, *Khoumani, Islamic Fundamentalists and the Contributions of Islamic Sciences to Modern Civilization*, Indiana: Foundations Press of Notre Dame, 1983.

23. Esposito, *Voices...*, pp. 8-9; Voll, *op. cit.*, p. 113; Esposito, "Islam in The...," pp. 126-127.

24. For a state by state listing of organizations, groups and leaders see Robin Wright's study.

25. See: Walter H. Capps, (ed.) *Ways of Understanding Religion*, N.Y.: The Macmillian Co., 1972.

26. Esposito, *Voices..*, p. 4-5; Taheri, *op. cit.*, pp. 10, 16, 30-31.

27. Farghal, *op. cit.*, p. 100.

28. Hanifi, *op. cit.*, p. 56.

29. Sardar, *op. cit.*, p. 8.

30. Esposito, *Voices...*, p. 79.

31. Farhang and Montavalli, *op. cit.*, pp. 19-20.

32. See: Tarif Khalidi, "The Idea of Progress in Classical Islam," *Journal of Near Eastern Studies*, October 1981, vol. 40, no. 4, pp. 277-289.

33. Esposito, *Voices...*, pp. 13-14, 33-35, 54-55, 222-223; Zonis, "Iran...," p. 591; M. Zonis and D. Brumberg, *Khomeini, The Islamic Republic of Iran, and The Arab World*, Mass.: Harvard Middle East Papers, (no. 5), 1987, p. 23; Taheri, *op. cit.*, p. 231.

34. See: Abd al-Rahman Azzam, *The Eternal Message of Muhammad*, N.Y.: Mentor Books, 1964, pp. 104-115; J. L. Esposito, *Islam and Politics*, Syracuse: Syracuse Univ. Press, 1984; Sardar, *op. cit.*, pp. 126-127.

35. Esposito, *Voices...*, p. 154.

36. Taheri, *op. cit.*, p. 17.

37. Esposito, *Voices...*, p. 252.

38. As put to me by an islamic fundamentalist cleric, "a physically deformed, mentally retarded black women will achieve the presidency of South Africa, under Apartheid, before the best qualified Christian or woman will head an Islamic state."

39. Esposito, *Voices...*, p. 5; Farghal, *op. cit.*, pp. 104-105; Voll, *op. cit.*, pp. 115-116.

40. Abraham, *Islam and Christianity...*, pp. 58-59; Pipes, *op. cit.*, p. 492.

41. Hanifi, *op. cit.*, p. 57.

42. *Ibid.*, p. 57; *International Institute of Islamic...*, pp. 7-8.

43. Bassam Tibi, "Neo-Islamic Fundamentalism," in *Development*, 1987, no. 1, p. 66.

44. For more on this procedure see: Mohammad Khalid Masud, *Islamic Legal Philosophy*, Pakistan: Islamic Research Institute, 1977, pp. 173-185; Sardar, *op. cit.*, pp. 75, 113; Taylor, *op. cit.*, p. 120.

45. On the fundamentalist view of Israel see: Esposito, *Voices...*, p. 217.

46. On Lebanese communal relations and the civil war see: A. J. Abraham, *Lebanon: A State of Siege (1975-1984)*, IN.: Wyndham hall Press, 1984.

47. Taheri, *op. cit.*, p. 128, 204; Nahas, *op. cit.*, p. 522; Wright, *op. cit.*, p. 65; Zonis and Blumberg, *op. cit.*, pp. 55-62.

48. Hanifi, *op. cit.*, p. 58; Pipes, *op. cit.*, p. 940; Taylor, *op. cit.*, p. 121; Esposito, *Voices...*, pp. 81-82.

49. Esposito, "Islam in the Politics...," p. 53; Esposito, *Voices...*, p. 63; Hanifi, *op. cit.*, p. 58; Wright, *op. cit.*, p. 60, 120.

50. A. J. Abraham, "The Theory and Practice..., p. 21.

51. *Ibid.*.

52. Quoted from Wright's *Sacred Rage*.

CHAPTER ONE

THE DOCTRINE OF JIHAD

The term Jihad is derived from the verb jahada (abstract noun juhd); it signifies the use or exertion of one's utmost power, efforts, endeavors, or his ability in contending with an enormous object. The object of jihad can take any one or more of the following forms: a visible enemy, the devil, or one's self, all of which are indicated in the Quran:

> And Strive in His cause
> As ye ought to strive
> He has chosen you, and has
> Imposed no difficulties on you
> In religion; it is the cult
> Of your father Abraham
> It is He Who has named
> You Muslims, both before
> And in this
> That the Apostle may be
> A witness for you, and ye
> Be witnesses for mankind
> So establish regular prayer
> Give regular charity
> And hold fast to God
> He is your Protector...   (Q 22:78)

Thus the judicial and theological meaning of jihad projects an exertion of one's power in God's cause (fi sabel Allah), to spread God's religion (Islam) to every one and everywhere.

> ...Ye strive
> In the cause of God
> With your property
> And your person...   (Q 61:11)

In the broad sense, the word jihad is not restricted to war or combat, since the word "strive" in the cause of God may be achieved by both peaceful or violent means or a combination of both. It may be regarded as a form of religious propaganda, and can be carried out by both persuasion or the sword (or modern weaponary).

> And if any strive
> they do so
> For their own souls...   (Q 29:6)

Jihad is also expressed in terms of one's salvation or as a purification of the soul, in a spiritual sense. In the Medinah revelations of the Quran, jihad is expressed in terms of strife and struggle.

> Those who believe
> And those who suffered exile
> And fought
> In the path of God...   (Q 2:218)

Thus, the jurists have distinguished between four different ways in which Moslems may fulfill their obligation for jihad:

1. Jihad of the heart (faith)
2. Jihad of the tongue (speech)
3. Jihad of the hand (good works)
4. Jihad of the sword (holy war)

The first category is concerned with combating the temptation of sin. The Prophet Muhammad considered it to be the greatest Jihad.[1] The second and the third are mainly concerned with supporting the truth and correcting wrongs; the last is precisely equivalent to the meaning of holy war, and it is concerned with fighting the enemies of God, the polytheists and other enemies of Islam. This is regarded as the lesser jihad[2] and includes any war between Moslems and non-Moslems, under the direction of Islamic law: "Undertaken by civilized peoples and leaders in order to defend the religion and preserve the established order,"[3] and, it follows that "Jihad in the technology of law is used for expanding ability and power in the fighting in the path of God by means of life, property, tongue, and other than these."[4]

Consequently, the doctrine of jihad is restricted to religious wars, for all wars in Islam, defensive or offensive, are religious. There is no concept of a secular war; anyone who attacks Islam by word or deed, or offers an alternative to Islamic laws or culture, makes war upon God, and, this will result in the call for jihad.

The Emergence of The Doctrine of Jihad

War was in existence among the Arab tribes long before the advent of Islam. Since each tribe formed a separate and independent unit, its independence extended to the individual as well. Each person recognized the authority and leadership of his own chief. The tribes often fought each other for power and prestige.

Pagan Arabia also suffered from the impact of polytheism; thus cruel wars for revenge and vendetta ridden struggles left Arabia politically unstable. According to the well known Arab sociologist, Ibn Khaldoun, the state of affairs that had developed among the Arabs included a powerful spirit of self-reliance, courage, and at times co-operation among tribal members.

On the negative side, however, these conditions intensified and elevated the characteristics of warfare, competition, and rivalry among the Arabians and it created a state of insecurity and instability, rife with violence.

Arabia was ready for revolution under new and strong leadership when the Prophet Muhammad proclaimed the message of Islam. It was welcomed by many despite the objections of some of the members of his own tribe. Nevertheless, within a short period of time, Muhammad exercised both temporal and religious power over Arabia. Unity was imposed; and it ended the family and blood ties replacing them with ties of faith and brotherhood. But, more important, the Islamic state redirected the warlike spirit of the Arabians away from petty conflicts to thoughts of war for the faith.

Jihad as Righteous War

War is considered righteous in Islam when it is waged for justifiable reasons in accordance with the laws (the Shari'ah) of Islam and the morals of the society.

Ancient Israel looked upon war as sanctified and dedicated to God whom they conceived of as a "Man of War" who was "Mighty in battle" and "the Lord of hosts, the God of the armies of Israel."[5] Clearly, to the Jews, war was holy. God gave them the land of Canaan, and thus, war became a duty to evict the previous settlers. The warrior's were to remove "evil" from their midst and replace it with the "house of Israel."

Similarly, the doctrine of jihad in Islam is propagated to establish justice, peace, and order to bring the world to God's faith, by submission. This is clearly stated by the Prophet Muhammad who said: "I am ordered to fight the polytheists until they say there is no God but Allah."[6] Consequently, Islam abolished all wars except those in the path of God. Moslem nations, however, were involved in wars among themselves contrary to the teaching of the faith. Those wars were justified by claiming that they are waged to preserve Islam from the corruption of hypocritical rulers. The Quran urges all believers to make peace among themselves[7] for they are brothers;[8] they should wage war against the unbeliever,[9] until they become believers,[10] saving only the souls which God has permitted to live.[11]

In Moslem legal theory, Islam and *Shirk* (associating other gods with Allah) can not be reconciled:

> ...believers, listen not
> To the Unbelievers, but strive
> Against them with the utmost...   (Q 25:52)

so that it is permitted to:

> ...fight those who believe not
> In God nor the Last Day...
> Nor acknowledge the Religion
> Of Truth.   (Q 9:29)

It is the ultimate fate of the Moslem community to root out all evil or corruption in order to establish Islamic principles of justice. To achieve that goal, the jihadist must "fight against the friends of Satan" (Q 4:76), and for "the cause of God, but transgress not" (Q 9:20), "kill not the soul which God has prohibited" (Q 25:68), "but if the enemy is inclined towards peace, so thou incline" (Q 8:61).

This sacred jihad offers the participant a noble promise of martyrdom and eternal life in paradise immediately and without trial upon resurrection on the Day of Judgement:

Think not of those
Who are Slain in God's way
As dead. Nay they live
Finding their sustenance
In the Presence of their Lord.   (Q 3:169)

It is said that Muhammad assured a women whose son was killed in the battle of Badr that he was in the highest heaven.[12] Furthermore, he declared that "there are one hundred stages in Paradise that are provided by Allah for those who fight for His path."[13]

Also, jihad is the Islamic instrument to carry out, expand, the Moslem belief-system in the unity of God and the prophethood of Muhammad;[14] it places dar al-Islam (the Moslem World) in a permanent state of struggle with dar al-harb (the non-Moslem World), until it is reduced to non-existence.[15]

In order for the Moslem state to defend itself and be able to extend its faith, it must be militarily prepared to raise its armies immediately. This duty falls to the head of state, the Commander of the Believers, who must declare a universal jihad binding upon all Moslems, including women, children and the aged.[16] Thus, jihad is a precursor of today's "people's war."

Jihad in Islam is obviously a collective obligation of the whole community transcending location and nationality. It binds and unites all believers together against all other religions and political ideologies.[17] From the Islamic point of view, Islam must replace all other religions and political systems[18] and distance or citizenship must never separate believers or diminish their cause of world-wide Islamification. This does not always imply force since the Quran states that "there is no compulsion in religion," (Q 2:256) but jihad can be achieved by persuasion, negotiation, conviction and any other peaceful means. However, the fact remains that for polytheists they must accept Islam or fight against it. They can not reject it and go their way.

The Shi'ite and Kharij'ite Doctrine of Jihad

For the Shi'ite sect, the doctrine of jihad is declared on both Moslems and non-Moslems who do not obey Islam.[19] Jihad is regarded as one of the chief functions of the Imamate (Shi'ite clergy). The leading Imam is regarded as an infallible ruler, and only he can declare a jihad. He can come to terms with his enemies or seek the support of non-Moslems but only on a temporary basis to avoid defeat. The disappearance of the last Imam in 878 A.D. has left the duty of declaring jihad technically unfulfilled. According to Shi'ite legal theory, the struggle is now dormant or in a state of suspension, until the reappearance of the missing Imam. He will return as the Mahdi (the Guide) ushering in an age of absolute (Islamic) justice.[20] Until then, the Shi'ite clergy rules on his behalf in a caretaker capacity.

In contrast to the Shi'ite sect, the Kharji sect maintains that jihad is a fundamental article of faith that can never be abandoned. It is the sixth pillar of the faith.[21] Their argument is based upon the idea that the Prophet Muhammad spent most of his life in a state of jihad, consequently, all believers should follow his example. The state must be prepared to wage jihad at all times, with or without an existing Imam. Thus, it is incumbent upon the individual believer as a personal duty. This is the current view of today's fundamentalists.

The Kharij'ite doctrine of jihad prefers strife and violence to peaceful propaganda. For them, belief in Islam must be accepted without argument, so that all evil and injustice can end. The use of warfare was sanctioned by the prophet who said: "My fate is under the shadow of my spear."[22] Apparently, the spirit of tolerance in Islam made little impact upon the Kharij'ites who were described as fanatics and brutal in their treatment of prisoners, including women and children, taken in war.[23]

Today, the polytheists have disappeared from the Middle East leaving only Jews and Christians as non-believers. They live under precarious conditions, stressing their nationalism to win acceptance in the Middle East. But they are still seen by the fundamentalists as second class citizens. Beyond the Middle East, the war goes on for the fundamentalists who seek worldwide conversion to Islam. And, they continue to fear the imposition of foreign ideologies that vie for the mind's of Islam's youth.

NOTES

1. Abu Muhammad Ali Ibn Ahmed Ibn Hazam, *Kitab al-Fasl fi al-Milal wa al-Ahwa al-Nihal*, Cairo, 1321 A.H., vol. 4, p. 135.

2. Muhammad Ibn Isa al-Tirmidhi, *Sahih al-Tirmidhi (Tirmidhi's Sahih)*, Cairo, 1931, vol. 7, p. 122.

3. Franz Rosenthal, "State and Religion According to Abu al-Hasen al-Amri," in *The Islamic Quarterly*, vol. 3, no. 1, April, 1956, p. 49.

4. Muhammad Hamidullah, *The Muslim Conduct of State*, Lahore, India: Kashmiri Bazar Pub., 1945, p. 191.

5. Ex. 15:2; Psalm 24:9.

6. Ya'qub Ibn Ibrahim al-Ansari Abu Yusuf, *Kitab al-Kharaj*, Cairo: Salfich Press, 1246 A.H., p. 213.

7. Q 49:9.

8. Q 49:10.

9. Q 8:65.

10. Q 49:9.

11. Q 25:52.

12. Abu Abd Allah Muhammad Ibn Ismail al-Bukhari, *Kitab al-Jami al-Sahih (Bukhari's Sahih)*, ed. M. Ludolf Krehl, Leiden, 1864, vol. 2, p. 202.

13. *Ibid.*, p. 200.

14. Abu Da'ud, *Sunan*, Cairo, 1935, vol. 3, p. 4.

15. Q 8:60.

16. Bukhari's *Sahih*, vol. 3, p. 218. Those who are not capable of fighting have to support the army with arms and ammunition, and take care of the wounded.

17. The purpose of community participation in the jihad was to make it the state's responsibility.

18. The idea that Islam would replace all other religions is expressed in the hadith of the prophet.

19. Majid Khadduri, *War and Peace in The Law of Islam*, Baltimore: Johns Hopkins Press, 1955, p. 66.

20. *Ibid.*, p. 67.

21. The pillars of the faith are: bearing witness, prayer, alms giving, fasting, and pilgrimage to Mecca.

22. Bukhari's *Sahih*, vol. 2, p. 227.

23. Abu al-Fath al-Shahrastani, *Kitab al-Milal wa al-Nihal*, London: Cureton Pub., 1846, pp. 90-93.

CHAPTER TWO

TYPES OF JIHAD

Moslem jurists and theologians distinguished between jihad against polytheists, pantheists, and atheists, and jihad against the People of The Book (Jews and Christians) who believe in God but not in the prophethood or message of Muhammad. Among Moslems jihad is sanctioned against apostates and dissenters from the faith, for there is no conversion from Islam. Each of the above parties was treated differently. Some Islamic schools of law restricted jihad to only the polytheists, apostates, thieves and dissenters.[1] Others believed that based upon the Quran and the speech of the prophet, Islam must be imposed upon all peoples.[2] The majority of jurists and theologians believe that the prophet approved jihad against all nations without restrictions.[3] In the Middle Ages, the Islamic authorities established an additional form of jihad to protect the borders known as the jihad of the "ribat" (outpost).[4] These are the four catagories of jihad.

Jihad Against Polytheists

To associate God with any person, place or thing is the greatest sin in Islam and those who believe this are called mushrikun (ascribing partners to God) or polytheists.[5] For their beliefs they are regarded in the Quran as the absolute enemies of God.

Islam can in no way associate or reconcile itself with polytheists for they are unpardonable sinners; believers should avoid them and should not even pray for them, even if they are their nearest relatives.[6] On at least one occasion, the Prophet Muhammad displayed sympathy towards them and prayed for them, but at other times he cursed them calling down fire upon them, earthquakes and other calamities. Marriage between Moslems and pagans are forbidden, because they are sinners and unclean, and their idols can not intercede for them with God.[7]

The term "shirk" is similar to that of "kufr" (disbelief) which includes both the mushrikun and the People of the Book,[8] but it is reserved in the Quran for polytheism and not for Jews and Christians. In the speech of the prophet (the Hadith) the term shirk is used to indicate "an external thing obscuriing the belief in the oneness of God."

Muhammad's policy, as well as that of his successors, was to invite the non-believers to accept Islam before waging war against them. Nevertheless, all Moslems are under an eternal obligation to "kill the idolators wherever they find them."[9]

Jihad Against Apostasy

Apostacy in Islamic law means turning away from Islam, after accepting it, even if the acceptance is under duress. If the convert refuses to accept every article of the faith, he is declared an apostate.[10]

Islam does not distinguish between an apostate who was born of Moslem parents or a convert to the faith. The intention of any Moslem, born to the faith or convert, to accept another religion is sufficient to declare him an enemy of God and to wage a jihad against him. Apostasy is an unpardonable act, for there is no freedom of religion in Islam nor is there room for conscience objection in the faith. Muhammad is reported to have said: "kill he who changes his religion,"[11] and, on another occasion, he said," fight them that there be no sedition and that the religion may be God's...."[12]

Nevertheless, all Moslem jurists in all the schools of law have agreed that before prosecuting and condemning the apostate he may be given one last chance to recant and remove any doubts he may harbor in regard to his beliefs.[13] The apostate, however, remains under threat of execution until he reaccepts Islam.[14]

As a general rule, a female apostate may not be condemned to death, but, rather, she may be jailed and beaten until she returns to the fold. (According to al-Mawardi's thesis on this, he claims that the prophet killed an appostate woman named um Ruman.)[15] The Hanifi school of law maintains that an apostate woman may be condemned into slavery and treated as a spoil of war; the same rule applies to apostate children. The other schools of law do not approve of these stern measures.

An apostate has no place to live, since he is outside the Moslem community, nor can he be regarded as a protected person (a dhimi/Jew or Christian); the poll tax is not accepted from him for his protection. He must accept Islam or the challenge of jihad.[16] If he escapes to a non-Moslem territory, his property and all his belongings will revert to the Moslem community, until he recants. Otherwise, his possessions will be distributed among his Moslem heirs as if he were dead. His debts will be terminated,[17] since the Moslem community can not be responsible for the debts of non-Moslems.

Jihad Against The People of The Book

The People of The Book includes Jews, Christians and Sabians. These people believe in one God but not in Muhammad and the Quran. Therefore, from the Moslem perspective, they are partial believers who have distorted their original scriptutres. When God sent His last prophet and messenger to guide them to the truth, they rejectd him, but remained monotheists. For those reasons, they are liable only for partial punishment. Thus, jihad is invoked against them, but not to the same degree as it is pressed against pagans who must choose between conversion or extinction.

The scripturaries are offered the choice between Islam, a poll tax (a fine), or jihad. If they choose Islam, they are entitled to full civil and human rights in the Moslem state. If they accept the tax, they are protected but lose much of their rights. If they accept jihad, they are treated as polytheists, for becoming allies against God.

Jihad Against Heretics

A heretic may form his own group provided that he will not renounce the authority of the religious leaders or attack accepted Islamic beliefs. Under those conditions, he may reside in dar al-Islam and express his views.[18] But, if he rebels against the law, he will find himself in a state of jihad with the authorities.

Jihad Against Deserters and Highway Robbers

Acts of theft or robbery committed by Moslems are regarded as serious sins against the community and state and, more importantly against God. Therefore, God has legislated the punishment:

> The punishment of those
> Who wage war against God
> And His Apostle, and strive
> With might and main
> For mischief through the land
> Is: execution, or crucifixion
> Or the cutting off of hands
> And feet from opposite sides
> Or exile their disgrace
> In this world, and
> A heavy punishment is theirs
> In the Hereafter;   (Q 5:36)

Thus, civil crimes are also religious crimes that the state[19] may wage jihad against. The legal authorities have the prerogative to treat the criminal as a dissenter from the faith,[20] for law, faith and state are intertwined in Islam.

Jihad of the Ribat

A ribat for safeguarding the frontiers of an Islamic state is a building or fortress established near its harbors or borders. It is sanctioned in both the Quran and the Hadith. The Prophet Muhammad is quoted as having said: "One day and night of Ribat is worth more than the fasting of one month..." and, on another occasion, he said,"... spending one night in a ribat is worth more than a thousand spent in prayer."[21]

§ § §

NOTES

1. Ali Ibn Muhammad al-Mawardi, *Kitab al-Ahkam al-Sultaniyya*, Cairo, 1909, pp. 29, 50.

2. Q 62:11.

3. Abu Yusuf, *op. cit.*, p. 213; Abu Da'ud, *op. cit.*, vol. 3, p. 44.

4. Roger Le Tourneau, *The Almohad Movement in North Africa in the Twelfth and Thirteenth Centuries*, New Jersey: Princeton Univ. Press, 1969.

5. Q 6:49.

6. Q 9:113.

7. Q 6:93; 10:18.

8. Q 98:5.

9. Q 9:5; 9:123.

10. Al-Mawardi, *op. cit.*, pp. 44-45; 30-31.

11. *Ibid.*, p. 45.

12. Q 2:193.

13. Abu Yusuf, *op. cit.*, p. 216.

14. *Ibid.*, p. 217.

15. Al-Mawardi, *op. cit.*, p. 45.

16. Abu Yusuf, *op. cit.*, p. 216.

17. Al-Mawardi, *op. cit.*, p. 45.

18. *Ibid.*, p. 48.

19. Al-Mawardi, *op. cit.*, pp. 50-51.

20. *Ibid.*, p. 51.

21. Bukhari's *Sahih*, vol. 2, p. 222.

CHAPTER THREE

THE POLICY OF JIHAD

When Islam expanded throughout Arabia, the doctrine of jihad greatly influenced the believers; they felt it was their duty to fight in the path of God. In practice, however, this was not practical for both physical and economic reasons. Therefore, the Moslem community was divided into two groups: those who were able to wage jihad, and those who could not but could contribute to the effort by supplying arms, ammunition, and other necessities of war including caring for the wounded.

The jihadist must also possess certain qualifications in order to enable him to carryout his duty. First, above all else, they must be true believers in God and His prophet. Both the Maliki and Shafa'i law schools support this requirement and maintain that Muhammad rejected the aid of non-believers. The Hanifi law school rejects that assertion, saying that non-believers fought with the Moslems in the Battle of Qadisiyya,[1] in support of the Islamic state.

Secondly, physical health was important. The jihadist must be mature, of sound mind and an able bodied male. However, if an Islamic state comes under sudden attack, then all Moslems may join the holy jihad including women, children, and the aged. Only slaves were exempt, unless given their freedom.[2]

Lastly, the jihadist must be economically independent, so that he can support himself and his family during the war.

The main purpose of jihad is to expand the Islamic World. War was not for booty; it was for God. But, jihadists had to be paid for their services, hence the spoils of war were distributed after victory, according to a pre-determined formula.[3]

The jihadist was to conduct himself as a gentleman, be honest and straightforward as befits a soldier in God's army. He was forbidden to commit atrocities or to mutilate the dead enemy. As a jihadist, his life was committed to bringing victory to the army of God. Victory is always from God; yet the Moslem army could lose a battle, but could never be defeated.

The jihadist must be courageous and never retreat unless he is over-powered by an enemy and threatened with extinction.[4]

Before the war would start, a warning was due in accordance with the Quranic ideal for jihad: "Nor would we visit with our wrath until we had sent an Apostle" (to give warning).[5] This policy was continued by the prophet's successors in their wars with Byzantium and Persia.[6] The following letter[7] was sent by the famous Arab commander Khalid ibn al-Walid to the people of al-Mada'n:

> From Khalid Ibn al-Walid to the Persian authorities, peace be upon those that follow the path of truth. Thanks be to Allah who humiliated you and caused the collapse of your kingdom...those who pray our prayer and eat our meals are Moslems and will have the same rights as us. After you receive my letter send me guarantees and you will have peace; otherwise, in the name of Allah, I shall send you men who enjoy death as much as you like life.

If peaceful capitulation was achieved, Islamification followed; negotiations, in most cases, were limited to the release of prisoners, the signing of truces, the surrendering of a number of towns and cities, or the signing of a formal peace treaty.[8]

The Conduct of Fighting

The Isrealites consulted their God (Yaweh) regarding their battles and, they believe that He advised them about the proper time to begin their attack. Before the attack, they usually attempted to negotiate with their enemies, seeking their surrender,[9] to minimize bloodshed and destruction.[10] God sanctioned the Isrealite concept of war; burnt offerings were presented to Him for a quick victory. They carried the ark of the covenant before them to battle as a symbol of victory.[11]

Similarly, the early Christian armies and the Crusaders carried the Cross into battle as a symbol of triumph. In the Middle Ages, the Roman Church declared the "Truce of God" to limit warfare, in memory of Christ's passion from Wednesday evening in Holy Week until the following Monday morning.

Like the Israelites and early Christians, the jihadists abstained from war during their sacred months:

> But when the sacred months are passed away,
> Kill the idolators wherever ye may find them,
> and besiege them, and lie in wait for them in
> every place of observation...   (Q 9:5)

According to Islamic custom, the commander of the Moslem armies would ask the clergy to recite Quranic passages regarding jihad to the troops to encourage them,[12] for "there is no strength or power but in Allah."[13]

The rules of engagement with the enemy were formalized during the reign of the prophet's first successor, Caliph Abu Bakr, who addressed the troops on the Syrian border saying:[14]

> Stop, O people that I may give you ten rules to keep by heart! Do not commit treachery, nor depart from the right path. You must not mutilate, neither kill a child or aged man or woman. Do not destroy a palm tree, nor burn it with fire, and do not cut down any fruitful tree. You must not slay any of the flock or herds or the camels, save for your subsistence. You are likely to pass people who have devoted their lives to monastic service; leave them to that which they have devoted their lives. You are likely to find people who will present you meals of different kinds. You may eat; but do not forget to mention the name of God.

Moslem jurists, in general, agreed that non-combatants, such as women and children, and the sick and aged, should not be harmed. Some Islamic scholars, however, did disagree, saying that all polytheists could be killed. On the question of non-Moslem holy men, there was much controversy. Some jurists forbid killing them because they are peaceful people, while others approved jihad against them saying that they might instruct their co-religionists in defense of their faith which might hamper the spread of Islam.[15] The prophet's policy was not to harm women and children unless they fought against the Moslems.[16] And, later, Hanifi and Shafi'i jurists excluded peasants and merchants not engaged in fighting from the jihad.[17]

Moslem law prohibited excessive acts of brutality or inhumane treatment of prisoners, or the use of poisoned arms.[18] Only the Malikite school of law which dominates the Persian Gulf and Indian Ocean region approved the use of poisoned weapons.

And, lastly, foreign spies were killed and Moslem traitors were subject to severe punishment.[19]

§ § §

NOTES

1. Abu Ja'far Muhammad Ibn Jarar al-Tabari, *Ta'rikh al-Rasul wa al-Muluk*, ed. M. J. de Goeje, Leiden, 1893, series 1, vol. 4, p. 2261. (The unbelievers numbered about 12,000, some of whom accepted Islam after the battle.)

2. Abu Abd Allah Muhammad Idris al-Shafi'i, *Kitab al-Umm*, Cairo 1321-1325 A.H., vol. 4, p. 85.

3. Al-Midani, *Al-Lubab fi al-Sharh al-Kitab*, Cairo, 1955, vol. 1, p. 258. (One fifth of the spoils went to the treasury, the other four-fifths was divided among the jihadists, two shares went to the horsemen, one share to the infantry.)

4. To achieve martyrdom and instant entrance into paradise, one must die fighting the enemies of God.

5. Q 17:15.

6. Abu Yusuf, *op. cit.*, p. 118.

7. Al-Tabari, *op. cit.*, vol. 1, p. 2020.

8. Khadduri, *op. cit.*, p. 118.

9. II Kings 14:8. The only instance in which war was declared in Judaism without negotiations was the war between Amaziah, king of Judah and Jehoas, king of Israel.

10. Judges 11:12-28.

11. Deuteronomy 20:2-4.

12. At the head of each column, a clergyman would read a verse from the Quran regarding war to encourage the troops.

13. Al-Tabari, *op. cit.*, vol. 1, pp. 2294-2295.

14. *Ibid.*, p. 1850.

15. Al-Mawardi, *op. cit.*, p. 34.

16. *Ibid..*

17. Khadduri, *op. cit.*, p. 104.

18. *Ibid..*

19. *Ibid.*, p. 107.

CHAPTER FOUR

THE SPOILS OF WAR

The term spoil (ghanima) is applied specifically to property taken by the Moslems after the defeat, full or partial, of their enemies. It includes both movable and immobile property; it includes prisoners of war, including women and children. All spoils were divided among those men who took part in the battle, even if they did not get the opportunity to actually fight.

From the legal point of view, defeat alienates the enemy's right to ownership. Four-fifths of the booty was given to the warriors; one fifth of the spoils taken went to the treasury (bayt al-mal). Cavalry men could claim a share three times as large as that of the foot soldier.[1] (The Hanifite jurists alloted only a double amount to the cavalry). The Quran is unclear on the actual distribution of the booty:[2]

> Know that a fifth of what ye have belongs to Allah...to His Apostle,
> his family, to the orphans, the needy, and the traveler...

The Hanifites recognize only three catagories: the orphan, the needy, and the traveler, as mentioned in the Quran (Q 8:42). The portion originally allotted to the prophet is to be applied to the general good of the Moslem community.[3]

Immovable property posed a serious problem for the conquerors. During the life time of the prophet, land taken in battle was divided between the state and the jihadist. After the prophet's death, the Caliph Omar decided to impose a land tax (kharaj) on the newly acquired land, and the jizya on its inhabitants.[4] The Maliki law school considered all immovable property as public property owned by the state, for public revenue.

The fate of prisoners of war was based upon the following Quranic precept:

> It has not been fitting for any prophet
> To have captives until he has subdued
> the land...   (Q 8:67)

Islamic law, as interpreted by some scholars, allows the Imam to execute some or all of the captives,[5] or to ransom them, or to set them free, or to arrange a prisoner exchange. Moslem prisoners must do their best to escape, or to try to destroy the enemy's property. However, if they give a pledge of co-operation they must abide by it.[6]

Prisoners as Slaves

Slavery existed in pre-Islamic Arabia and the institution continued into the Islamic Age. Islamic slavery appears in a milder form than Greek or Roman slavery; perhaps, it was similar to the state of slavery among the Hebrews. Only Christianity, among the western religions, forbids slavery to its followers, according to the teachings of St. Paul in his statement to the Galatians.

In the Middle East, the Arabs took slaves by force as prisoners of war. Some were also purchased from foreign lands. As a general rule, the Arabs did not enslave fellow Arabs, although the Prophet Muhammad did enslave the Banu Mustaliq tribe. Arab slavery was primarily an intra-racial affair while blacks were enslaved in sub-Saharan Africa.

A master was permitted, under Islamic law, to use female slaves as concubines, but any children from such a union would be a free Moslem. If the master does not acknowledge fatherhood, the child remains a slave. Conversion to Islam may free a slave, but in some cases it was withheld.

A Christian or any other non-Moslem is not permitted to have a Moslem slave. A Moslem is a superior being, spiritually and culturally (some theologians add mentally as well), and thus can never be subject to the inferior non-believers. If a slave adopts Islam, his non-Moslem master is obligated to free him.

NOTES

1. Shafi'i, *op. cit.*, vol. 4, p. 64.

2. Abu Yusuf, *op. cit.*, p. 146.

3. Shafi'i, *op. cit.*, p. 64.

4. Abu Yusuf, *op. cit.*, p. 146.

5. *Ibid.*, pp. 195-196.

6. Muhammad Ibn Hassan al-Shaybani, *Kitab al-Siyar al-Kabir*, Hydera-bad, 1335 A.H., vol. 4, pp. 223-225.

CHAPTER FIVE

DIVISION OF THE WORLD

Moslem law binds individuals, not territorial groups. Moslems must always observe this characteristic of their faith wherever they reside. There are codes of conduct that govern a Moslem's behavior, his way of life, regardless of his physical location. A non-Moslem living in the Moslem World is bound by Islamic law, and is under the obligation to respect it, for God's law always supercedes man's law.

In Moslem constitutional law, the world is divided into two parts the Moslem World (dar al-Islam) and the non-Moslem World (dar al-harb). Any territory in which Islamic authority is manifest and the non-Moslems (the dhimmis) have accepted a subordinate position in relation to the Moslems is part of dar al-Islam.[1] A wider interpretation of this maintains that dar al-Islam is any territory where Moslems freely practice their faith and celebrate their feasts.

When a territory is conquered and incorporated into the Moslem World a specific sign of capitulation was placed on the pulpit of the mosque, signifying its consecration to God. If it was taken by force, a sword was placed on the pulpit; otherwise a wooden staff would be placed there to denote that the region surrendered peacefully. A wooden sword indicated that a city was taken by both force and non-violent means.

A land conquered by the armies of Islam may revert back to its former status if the Moslems residing there can no longer practice their faith, or if equality is achieved between Moslems and non-Moslems. The Hanifi jurists set down three additional conditions under which a Moslem state may lose its Islamic status:

1. When legal decisions of the non-believers are accepted with or in place of Islamic law, the state falls back to its previous status.

2. If the country breaks away from the Moslem World with no Moslem state coming between them or:

3. The Moslem authorities can no longer protect the citizens of the state, the territory is considered open to war. Some legal scholars maintain that dar al-Islam is only territory under Islamic law. This has always been the fundamentalist view. However, Moslems should work for the implementation of Islamic law wherever they live and form sizable minorities.[2]

Classification of the Moslem World

Islam is a missionary religion, an ever expanding faith that has no limits. But like all religions, it has a focal point from which it radiates. Therefore, the Moslem scholars viewed our planet as consisting of three Islamic zones.[3]

The first zone is the *haram* (the place of security) or the nucleus of the faith, Mecca and, according to some scholars, Medinah. Called "the two harams," they represent Islam's first victories. Non-Moslems may not live there.[4]

The Hijaz region is next in importance for Moslems, because of its location and because the Islamic message was directed towards the surrounding hills there. Non-Moslems can travel in that region up to a period of three days. A non-believer can not be buried there because that would constitute permanent residency.[5]

The last zone constitutes the balance of the Moslem World, where Jews, Christians, and Sabians may reside.[6] Islamic law grants full rights to all Moslems and partial rights to non-Moslems living among them in dar al-Islam. The personality of the ruler is a major factor in the conditions under which non-believers live.

When a non-Moslem wishes to live in a Moslem state, he is classified as a musta'min (one who seeks protection), and he and his family may reside anywhere except in the area forbidden to non-Moslems. He will enjoy the protection of the authorities and must pay the poll tax; and, he must refrain from any activity that could be injurious to the state. If he is found to be a spy, he is liable for capital punishment.[7] If he commits a crime, he may remain but he is subject to Islamic justice.[8]

Classification of the Non-Moslem World

The abode of war is that part of the world that is not governed by Islamic law; it is regarded as enemy territory and it is the main objective of jihad. Although, theoretically, the Moslem World is in a constant state of jihad with the non-Moslem World, continual war is impractical. Therefore a truce (hudna) may exist for practical reasons and negotiations may proceed. If a treaty relation develops between them, the non-Muslem lands are classified as dar al-sulh or dar al-ahd, by some schools of Islamic law. While not under Moslem rule or Moslem law, they do not obstruct Moslems living there from fulfilling their religious obligations. A Moslem not residing in dar al-Islam is not obliged to engage in any plan to strengthen the nation in which he lives, because it can never claim his true allegiance.[9] That allegiance belongs only to God and the world-wide Moslem community.

§ § §

NOTES

1. Abu Mansur Abd al-Qahir Ibn Tahir al-Baghdadi, *Kitab Usul al-Din*, Istanbul, 1928, p. 270.

2. Khadduri, *op. cit.*, pp. 28-29.

3. Al-Mawardi, *op. cit.*, pp. 141-143.

4. *Ibid.*, pp. 148-149.

5. *Ibid.*, p. 140.

6. *Ibid.*, pp. 154-155.

7. Abu Yusuf, *op. cit.*, p. 188.

8. Shafi'i, *op. cit.*, vol. 3, p. 326.

9. Shaybani, *op. cit.*, vol. 3, pp. 217-219.

CHAPTER SIX

JIHAD AND THE NON-MOSLEM SUBJECTS

According to Islamic law and custom, upon the conquest of new territories, the non-Moslem population that is not enslaved is guaranteed life and liberty, in a modified sense. They are known as Ahl al-Kitab (People of The Book) or Ahl al-Dhimmi (People of The Covenant) meaning Jews, Christians and Sabians. All others are termed *dahris*, an imprecise term found in Islamic literature used to denote "materialists" or "idolaters." They are subject to death or enslavement.

The dhimmis could be liable to support or serve in the Islamic army, for that would assist the expansion of Islam. However, Moslems should not aid or serve in non-Moslem armies, because that might impede the spread of Islam. Service in the military does not enhance a non-Moslem status as a citizen.

The Prophet Muhammad was both tolerant and kind in his relations with the dhimmis; his message was directed towards the pagans,[1] that they may believe in one God and in His messengers. Jews and Christians were already monotheists, but not full believers, having changed or corrupted their Scriptures (tahrif):[2]

> And for that they broke their covenant, We cursed them
> and placed in their hearts hardness, so that they
> perverted the words from their places and forgot a
> portion of what they were reminded of...   (Q 5:14)

Therefore, many Moslems believe that God commissioned Muhammad to lead the Jews and Christians back to the path of righteousness, and to re-establish God's laws and punishments among the Christians.

In an early treaty between the Jews of the Aws and Khadzaj tribes and the prophet, we see that the Jews were placed on an almost equal footing with the Moslems:[3]

> The Jews of Banu Aws form a nation with the believers. The Jews
> shall have their own religion, and the Moslems their own reli-

gion...No Jew is allowed to join the Moslems in battle without the authorization of Muhammad...The Jews shall contribute to the expense for battle so long as they fight with the believers...

The need for allies against the pagans may have been the compelling reason for an alliance with the Jews; but, once the prophet was successful in his wars, he never again required anything other than tribute for defense from the Scriptuary communities. He turned against them later, upholding the supremacy of Islam:

> Fight those who believe not in God nor the
> Last Day, nor hold that forbidden
> Which hath been forbidden by God and His Apostle
> Nor acknowledge the Religion Of Truth (even if they are)
> Of the People of The Book, Until they pay tribute
> With willing submission
> And feel themselves subdued...   (Q 9:29)

The Christians were obliged to pay the tribute (Jizyah/Jizya, poll tax) in return for freedom from molestation, as long as they maintained peaceful relations with the Islamic community.[4]

In another treaty between the prophet and the people of Najran, the Prophet Muhammad's attitude towards the non-Moslems is clarified:[5]

> They shall have the protection of Allah and the promise of Muhammad, the Apostle of Allah, that they shall be secured in their lives, property, lands, creed, those absent and those present, their families, their churches, and all that they possess...No hardships or humiliation shall be imposed on them nor shall their land be occupied by (our) army...

In return for the above considerations, the dhimmis agreed to provide the Moslems with financial aid and needed supplies.[6]

In a similar pact issued by Muhammad to the Christians of Ayla (Aqaba), the prophet offers them the conditions for peace:[7]

> To Yuhanna Ibn Ru'ba and the chiefs of the people of Ayla. Peace be upon you. Praise be to Allah, besides whom there is no God. I

shall not fight you until I have written you. Accept Islam, or pay the Jiza,...Honor the messengers and clothe them with good clothing...if you refuse, I will not accept anything from you until I have fought against you, and slain your men, and have taken captive (sabi) your women and children.

Yuhanna accepted the conditions laid down by the prophet and a pact was concluded between them. The prophet chose to negotiate with the dhimmis, perhaps in the hope that eventually they would accept Islam.

The Covenant of Umar (Omar)

Immediately after the death of the prophet, his successors, the caliphs, followed his policy towards the Scriptuaries; but, in time, as the Islamic state was consolidated, that policy was replaced by a legal program of overt and covert persecution and humiliation. The change in policy was in part responsible for what became known as the covenant of Omar, although some doubts regarding its authenticity have been observed. Different versions of the document have surfaced and contain legislation for conditions which had not yet arisen. Nevertheless, the documents represent Omar's policy, the Christians were:[8]

...not to build in Damascus and its environs churches, convents, chapels, monk's hermitages; not to repair what is dilapidated of their churches or any of them that are in Muslim quarters... to beat the naqus gently in churches; not to carry in processions a cross or (our) book; not to take out Easter or Palm Sunday processions... (and) to not resemble the Muslims in wearing the turban, shoes, nor in parting of the hair, nor in their way of riding; not to use their language nor be called by their names; to cut the hair in front and divide our forelock; to tie the zunnar (belt) around our waists; not to engrave Arabic on our seals; not to ride on saddles; not to keep arms nor put them in our houses, not wear swords...

Although the treaty bears the name of Caliph Omar, it was probably authored by his aid Abu 'Uaida, and ratified by him.

In another treaty attributed to the conquering hero Khalid ibn al-Walid given to the inhabitants of Damascus, the Christians were treated in a similar way. They were forbidden to display the cross in any gatherings, to strike a Moslem, to build new churches or to carry arms.[9] The treaty of Hims was similar to the others:[10]

> The inhabitants of Hims made peace with them on condition that he give them security for their persons, property, the city wall, the churches, and the mills. He set apart a quarter of the Church of St. John as a mosque, and imposed the tribute on those who remained.

The treaty of Jerusalem, believed to be the work of Omar, shows greater tolerance:[11]

> He gave them security for their lives, property, churches, and their crosses, their sick and healthy, and the rest of their religion...They shall not be persecuted for the sake of religion...There shall be no payment of tribute until the harvest is gathered...

These treaties were simple documents that were modeled on each other.[12] They are noted for their tolerance of the non-Moslem subjects, and, consequently, the Jews and Christians welcomed and supported the Moslems in their jihads against Byzantium and Persia. (In the battle of Yarmuk, twelve thousand Christians fought with the Moslem against the Byzantine forces.) This spirit of tolerance came at a time when the Moslems needed support from their subjects, but it soon changed once the Arab Empire swept away its enemies, expanding into the vital liimbs of Europe and the confines of Asia. Islamic law was enforced, and it became the major weapon in the Islamic arsenal for the conversion of the non-believers.

§ § §

NOTES

1. Q 5:4; 42:7; Abraham, *Islam and Christianity...*, p. v.

2. On tahrif see: Abraham, *Islam and Christianity...*, p. 87.

3. Abu Muhammad Abd al-Malik Ibn Hisham, *Kitab Sirat Sayyaduna Muhammad*, ed. Ferdinand Wustenfeld, Gottingin, 1858-1860, vol. 1, pp. 341-344.

4. Bukhari's *Sahih*, vol. 2, pp. 291-301.

5. Abu Yusuf, *op. cit.*, pp. 72-73; Abu al-Abbas Ahmad Ibn Jabir al-Baladhuri, *Kitab Futuh al-Buldan*, ed. M. J. de Goeje, Leiden, 1866, p. 65.

6. Clothing given to conquerors was taken by force.

7. Khadduri, *op. cit.*, pp. 180-181.

8. *Ibid.*, pp. 193-194.

9. Abu Yusuf, *op. cit.*, pp. 164-165; Al-Baladhuri, *op. cit.*, p. 121.

10. Al-Baladhuri, *op. cit.*, p. 121.

11. A. S. Tritton, *The Caliphs and Their non-Moslem Subjects*, London: Oxford Univ. Press, 1930, p. 10.

12. *Ibid.*, p. 12.

CHAPTER SEVEN

THE STATUS OF NON-MOSLEMS

Since the advent of Islam in the sixth century, a protracted struggle has ensued between the state (caliphs, sultans, kings, and presidents) and the legal establishment (the ulema/clergy and the Shari'ah courts) over the status of the non-Moslems (dhimmis), in the lands of Islam. In general, when the political forces were strong the dhimmis were tolerated, but when the legal establishment became more poweful, restrictions upon the dhimmis would increase. This situation has continued to the present time, with little change. The political forces continue to clash with the fundamentalists over the application and enforcement of Islamic injunctions upon the the non-Moslem community. Consequently, the conditions under which the dhimmis live was somewhat precarious. Often depending upon the personalities involved, the non-Moslems vacilated between prestige and degradation.

The Status of the Christians

During the early caliphate, the Christians lived under the general security that their poll tax granted them. Some prospered and attained high posts in the government, particularly when educated Moslems were too few. However, they were often replaced by Moslems when possible.

During the Umayyad Caliphate, under the reign of Mu'awiyah, Christians held several important positions. Al-Akhatal was the court poet; and the father of John of Damascus was the counselor to Caliph Abd al-Malik (686-705). Caliph al-Mutasim (833-842) employed two Christians who were brothers in his service. Salmuyah occupied a position similar to a modern secretary of state, and no royal documents were valid until he countersigned them. His brother, Ibrahim, was entrusted with the privy seal and he was the president of the public treasury. When he grew ill, the caliph would visit him at home; and when he died, a state funeral was held and the caliph was overcome with grief.

Caliph Abd al-Malik appointed an Edessan Christian named Athanasius to tutor his brother, Abd al-Aziz. During the reign of Caliph al-Mutadid (892-

902), Omar ben Yusuf became the first Christian governor of Anbar. Gabriel, the personal physician of Caliph Harun al-Rashid, was a Nestorian Christian.

As a community, the non-Moslems enjoyed a considerable amount of autonomy regarding their internal affairs; their religious authorities exercised judicial functions in personal family laws for the group. Only when Islam or Moslems were concerned, the Shari'ah was applied.

With the exception of churches and religious institutions in the major cities, churches and monasteries, for the most part, were independent of the state. The Hanifite jurists upheld the restrictions against building new churches, but they did allow some to be repaired when they were deemed a public hazard. The more intolerant Hanbalites made no concessions regarding the building or repair of churches.[1] Towns taken by force were not eligible to erect houses of prayer, unless a special treaty was made.[2] At about the same time in Egypt, the authorities permitted the Coptic Christian Church to erect new churches in Cairo,[3] and elsewhere. Churches were built during the reigns of Abd al-Malik, Yazid II, al-Mahdi (813-833), Haroun al-Rashid (786-809), al-Mamun (813-833) and others, with the consent of the state. Hisham Abd Allah al-Qasri, governor of Iraq, built a church to please his Christian mother and allowed Christians and Jews to construct houses of worship.[4]

Under the caliphs of Islam, the Nestorian Church[5] expanded its activities into Egypt, India and China. They were so effective in their missionary work that they won converts from among the Tartars.[6]

In general, the caliphs treated the various Christian sects equally and prevented them from persecuting one another.[7] The authorities did not favor any sect over the others for there was no purpose in that, because they were all misguided anyway. The Islamic religious leadership imposed upon the caliphs to put the non-believers in their place; and many of them began to issue edicts against the dhimmis. Several attempts were made to exclude the Christians from public office. Decrees were passed against them during the reigns of al-Mansur (745-775), al-Mutawakkil (847-861), al-Muqtaddir (908-932), and the Fatimid Caliph al-Amir (1101-1130). However, these proclamations were not always successful.

In addition to the prejudice the native Christians faced from the state and public, external conditions endangered their status within the Arab and Moslem empires. The fanaticism of the theologians worked against the dhimmis as well, but, perhaps, the main factor was political. The Moslems lost confidence and trust in the Christians because of their wars with Byzantium and with the Crusaders. (But despite the obvious political factors, some caliphs were disposed to act against the Christians. Al-Mutawakkil gave orders to demolish all churches and synagogues built after the Islamic conquests;[8] and Harun al-Rashid treated the dhimmis harshly and imposed a distinctive dress upon them; and, finally, al-Mansur removed all dhimmis from his administration.)

The Status of the Jews

Moslem sources do not mention much about the Jews; the law books rarely refer to them, speaking instead of dhimmis, presumably the Christians. Nevertheless, the Jews were engaged in important occupations such as doctors: civil servants, traders, and craftsmen. Apparently, they were too few in number.[9]

Even when the authorities persecuted the dhimmis, the Jews were not affected as much as the others. They were responsible to their own Chief Rabbi who was held in high esteem by the state and referred to by them as "Our Lord, the son of David." The Chief Rabbi's authority extended to all his co-religionists in the caliph's domain.[10]

The Status of the Sabians (Mandeans)

The Sabians, traditionally called the disciples of John the Baptist, are mentioned five times in the Quran:

> ...Those who believe, and those who follow are
> Jews or Christians or Sabians, whosoever believe
> in God and in the Last Day and work righteousness,
> shall have their reward...   (Q 2:62)

They paid the required poll-tax and received the customary protection of the Moslems. The Prophet Muhammad was friendly and co-operative towards them. He oftern referred to them as his friends.

The Status of the Magians (Zoroastrians)

Another group of tolerated people were the Magians. Mentioned only once in the Quran, in chapter two, verse 17, this sect acquired the status of dhimmis in the hadith and legal literature:[11]

> Umar, I was told of a people, worshippiing fire, who were neither Jews, nor Christians, nor people of the Book. He said that he did not know what to do with them. Then, Abd al-Rahman Ibn Auf said, I testify that the prophet said, "Treat them like the people of the Book."

Thus the Magians were treated like the people of the Book, and their temples, at first, did not suffer more than the churches. The Magians were forbidden to intermarry with the Moslems or to share meals with the conquerors.[12]

The Jizya/Jizyah

The jiza was a pre-Islamic practice in Arabia and the Fertile Crescent. The term jiza (in Aramaic, g z i tha) signified the difference between believers and non-believers,[13] among faiths.

It was a tax paid in cash or kind, excluding pigs, wine and dead animals, in the Islamic age. The tax was paid by those who could afford it, according to a fixed formula: the rich paid 48 dirhams a year, the middle class paid 24 dirhams per year and the poor paid only 12 dirhams annually.[14] The Moslem authorities exempted women: the very poor, children, the sick, monks and priests, unless they were wealthy. And, the tax collectors were told to refrain from harsh treatment for non-payment or slow payment.[15]

The jiza was paid in return for protection assumed by the state. When the people of Hira made their treaty with Khalid, they sought his protection from those who would oppress them.[16] Khalid was quoted as saying, "If we protect you, then the jiza is due us; but if we do not then it is not due."[17]

According to that agreement, the Moslems would return the full amount if they could not live up to their part of the contract.   When Emperor Heraclius raised a huge army to defeat the Moslems, Abu 'Ubaida ordered the return of the jiza. The Christians, fearing the return of the Byzantines and their heavy taxes, called the blessing of God upon the Moslems:[18]

> May God give you rule over us again and make you victorious over the Romans; had it been they, they would not have given us back anything, but would have taken all that remained with us.

Obviously, if a dhimmi converted to Islam, he would be exempt from the poll-tax or jiza, but he would still have to pay the land tax. As in the case of the Jurajimah, a Christian tribe near Antoich, if the dhimmis join the Moslem army, they were entitled to booty and were exempt from the jiza.[19]

The Age of Intolerance

Gradually, the adherents of Islam became vastly superior in number to any other faith. That great expansion was only partly the product of the sword. Jihad was only one factor in the expansion of the faith.

Among the dhimmis there were several groups that were only nominally Christians such as the Persian Shahrighans who believed that the Christ was only a prophet. They and other Unitarian groups converted to the new faith of the conquerors, seeing it as a completion of their own beliefs. Also, many Christians left the Orthodox Church having become tired of its confusing dogmatic controversies. And, lastly, some Christians defected from their faith because they believed that the hand of God was guiding the true believers (the Moslems) to world-wide victory.

In parts of Syria and in the Lebanon, the Moslem faith was seen as a new Christian heresy.   Particularly in the Lebanon, among the Maronite Christians, the differences between Islam and Christianity were seen as differences of interpretation rather than substance.   Thus, a healthy atmosphere developed between the two faiths, and the Christian Maronites were spared the status of dhimmi.   The two great faiths flourished in harmony, until the recent rise of Islamic fundamentalism.

As the Islamic state grew powerful, the dhimmis were no longer essential to the operation of the state; the Islamic clergy became more fundamentalist in its outlook, and the dhimmis began to experience social pressure to convert. The law courts did not favor them and they were viewed as outside the ideology of the state. They began to suffer persecution and humiliation, befitting a subject people. From the time of the collapse of the Abbasid Caliphate (1258 A.D.) to the present, the clergy has sought to put them in the proper Quranic place.

§ § §

NOTES

1. T. W. Arnold, *The Preaching of Islam*, London: Constable, 1913, p. 65.

2. *Ibid.*.

3. *Ibid.*, p. 86.

4. P. K. Hitti, *History of the Arabs*, New York: MacMillan and Co., 1951, p. 234.

5. John Joseph, *The Nestorians and their Muslim Neighbors,* New Jersey: Princeton Univ. Press, 1961.

6. Arnold, *op. cit.*, p. 68.

7. *Ibid.*.

8. Al-Tabari, *op. cit.*, vol. 3, p. 1390.

9. There were between 40,000 and 70,000 Jews in Alexandria Egypt at the time of the Arab conquest. Tritton, *op. cit.*, pp. 92-93.

10. Tritton, *op. cit.*, pp. 96-97.

11. Abu Yusuf, *op. cit.*, p. 74.

12. Baladhuri, *op. cit.*, p. 80.

13. Khadduri, *op. cit.*, p. 189.

14. On the jiza see: Muhammad Sa'id al-Almoudi, *Min Ta'rikhna*, Saudi Pub. House, 1967, p. 24.

15. Abu Yusuf, *op. cit.*, p. 96.

16. Al-Tabari, *op. cit.*, vol. 3, p. 2055.

17. *Ibid.*.

18. Arnold, *op. cit.*, p. 61.

19. Baladhuri, *op. cit.*, p. 159.

CONCLUSION

The doctrine of jihad is deeply rooted in the hearts and minds of all Moslems. Jihad is the main instrument to expand Islam throughout the entire world, and eventually make it the only religion of mankind. Until then, all Moslems must freely participate in some form of jihad because it is God's command to them. Clearly, Islam would not have achieved its great victories had it not been for the doctrine of jihad. Although originally for expansion of the faith, jihad also became a method to safe-guard the community from heresy or backsliding.

While jihad actually reoriented the war-like raiding spirit of the pagan Arabians into war for the faith, fighting was not the only proper means of jihad. The Prophet Muhammad realized that the message of God may be extended by both the sword and by persuasion, in order to instill true conviction among the new converts.

As the Islamic state or empire grew in power, the application of Islamic law began to change the conditions under which the Jews and Christians lived. At first tolerated by the powerful conquerors who needed their assistance to run the newly acquired territories, they were later subjected to intense humiliation and persecution. Nevertheless, the Christians in the Moslem World held high posts, fought in the army as jihadists, were economically successful and contributed to the European Renaissance.

The pagan were not as fortunate as the dhimmis. They were under constant jihad by the sword and the law. Their temples were destroyed or turned into mosques and they were under pain of death if they practiced, preached or exhibited their faith.

For the Christians, Islamic law imposed several restrictions. The testimony of a Christian against a Moslem required another Moslem's support. Churches had to be physically lower than mosques, and old churches could not be repaired. New churches could not be built. All religious ceremonies had to be low-keyed, and carrying the cross in a procession was prohibited. Christian men could not marry Moslem women. Eventually, many Christians converted to escape the law.

In time, Islam became a dominant world force, placing all Moslems under permanent obligation to carry the frontiers of the faith to new regions of the world, until every tongue declares that, "There is no God but God, and Muhammad is the messenger of God."

BIBLIOGRAPHY

Primary Sources

Abu Da'ud, (of al-Basrah), *Sunan (Traditions)*, Cairo, 1935.

Abu Yusuf, Ya'qub ibn Ibrahim al-Ansari, *Kitab al-Kharaj (The Book of Land Taxes)*, Cairo: Salfich Press, 1346 A. H..

Al-Baghadi, Abu Mansur Abd al-Qahir ibn Tahir, *Kitab Usul al-Din (Origins of the Faith)*, Istanbul, 1928.

Al-Baladhuri, Abu al-Abbas Ahmed ibn Yahya ibn Jabir, *Kitab Futuh al-Buldan (The Opening of Nations)*, ed. M. J. de Gjoeje, Leiden, 1866.

Al-Bukhari, Abu Abd Allah Muhammad ibn Isma'il, *Kitab al-Jami al-Sahih (Bukhari's Sahih/The Genuine)*, ed. M. L. Krehl. Leiden, 1865.

Al-Mawardi, Ali ibn Muhammad, *Kitab al-Akham al-Sultaniyya (The Book of Government Ordinances)*, Cairo, 1909.

Al-Midani, *Al-Lubab fi al-Sharh al-Kitab (The Essence in Quranic Commentary)*, Cairo, 1955.

Al-Quran (The Holy Qu-ran), A. Yusuf Ali's Translation.

Al-Shahrastani, Abu al-Fath, *Kitab al-Milal wa al-Nihal*, (The Book of Creeds and Sects), London: Cureton Pub., 1846.

Al-Shafi'i, Abu Abd Allah Muhammad Idris, *Kitab al-Umm (The Source Book)*, Cairo, 1321-1325 A. H..

Al-Tabari, Abu Jafar Muhammad ibn Jarir, *Ta'rikh al-Rasul wa al-Muluk (The Annals of the Apostle and Kings)*, ed. M. J. de Goeje, Series 1, 15 vol., Leyden, 1879-1901.

Al-Tirmidhi, Muhammad ibn Isa, *Sunan (Traditions)*, Cairo, 1931.

Al-Tirmidhi, Muhammad ibn Isa, *Sahih al-Tirmidhi (Tirmidhi's Sahih/The Genuine)*, 7 vol. Cairo, 1291.

Al-Zabadi, Al-Sayyid Muhammad Murtada al-Husayni, *Taj al-Arus (The Brides Crown)*, Cairo: Al-Khairiya Press, 10 vo., 1307.

Ibn Hanbal, Ahmad ibn Muhammad, *Al-Musnad (The Reference)*, Cairo, 6 vol., 1313.

Ibn Hazam, Abu Muhammad Ali ibn Ahmad, *Kitab al-Fasl fi al-Milal was al-Ahwa al-Nihal (The Book of Different Creeds and Sects)*, Cairo, 5 vol., 1347-1348 A. H..

Ibn Hisham, Abu Muhammad Abd al-Malik, *Kitab Sirat Sayyaduna Muhammad (A Biography of the Prophet Muhammad)*, ed. F. Wustenfeld, Gottingin, 2 vol. 1858-1860.

Malik ibn Anas, *Kitab al-Muwatta' (The Levelled Path)*, Cairo, 2 vol. 1939.

Malik ibn Anas, *Sharh al-Mana fi Ilm al-Usul (Commentary on the Meaning of Islam)*, Cairo, n.d..

Shaybani, Muhammad ibn Hassan, *Kitab al-Siyar al-Kabir (The Great Book of History)*, Hydarabad, 4 vol., 1335 A.H..

Secondary Sources (Arabic)

Abu Dahsh, Abd Allah ibn Muhammad ibn Hasyn, *Athr Dawat al-Shaykh Muhammad ibn Abd al-Wahab (The Effects of the Cause of Shaykh Muhammad ibn Abd al-Wahab)*, Dar al-Hukmat, Riyad, Saudi Arabia, 1985.

Al-Amoudi, Muhammad Sa'id, *Min Ta'rikhna (From Our History)*, Saudi Arabia: Saudi Pub. House, 1968.

Al-Ibadi, Abdal Hamid, *Al-Dawlah al-Islamiyah (The Islamic State)*, Cairo: Misri Press, 1954.

Al-Qawmiyah al-Arabiyah wa al-Islam (The Arab nation and Islam), Pub. by The Center For the Study of Arab Unity, Markaz Dirasat al-Wahdah al-Arabiyah, Beirut, 1984.

Al-Shira, Maluf, *Al-Harakat al-Islamiyya fi Lubnan (Moslem Political Movements in Lebanon)*, Beirut: Dar Sannin, 1984.

Al-Uthimin, Abd Allah al-Salih, *Al-Shaykh Muhammad ibn Abd Al-Wahab, Hayathu wa Fikrahu (The Life and Thoughts of Shaykh Muhammad ibn abd al-Wahab)*, 3rd, ed., Riyad, Saudi Arabi, 1986.

Amara, Muhammad, *Al-Fikr al-Qa'id lil Thawra al-Iraniyah (Dominant Thinking in the Iranian Revolution)*, Cairo, 1982.

Fadl Allah, Muhammad Husayn, *Al-Islam wa al-Mantiq al-Quwwa (Islam and the Logic of Power)*, Beirut: Al-Muassasa al-Jamiyya, 1981.

Ghamrawi, Muhammad Zahzani, *Al-Siraj al-Wahaj (The Shining Lamp)*, Cairo, 1933.

Harb, Rageb, *Din al-Islam Aqwa (Islam's Faith is Stronger)*, Beirut, 1983.

Husayn, Taha, *Al-Futuah al-Kubra (The Great Conquest)*, Egypt: Dar al-Ma'arif Press, n.d..

Mawdudi, Abu al-Ala, *Mujaz Ta'rikh Tajdid al-Din (A Short History of the Revivalist Movement in Islam)*, Trans. By al-Ashari, Lahore: Islamic Pub., 1976.

Qutb, Sayyid, *Hadha al-Din (This is the Faith)*, Cairo: Dar al-Qalaam, 1962.

Qutb, Sayyid, *Darasat Islamiyah (Islamic Studies)*, Cairo: Salfich Press, 1973.

Qutb, Sayyid, *Al-Salaam al-'Alami wa al-Islam (Universal Peace and Islam)*, Beirut: Dar al-Shuruq, 1974.

Radhwan, Fatahz, *Al-Jihad, Qanun al-Hayat (Jihad, The Law of Life)*, Cairo: 1973.

Yazid, Abd al-Azia, *Ahdaf al-Thwrat al-Islamiyah (Goals of The Islamic Revolution)*, Beirut, 1983.

Secondary Sources (English)

Abraham, A. J., "The Theory and Practice of Islamic Fundamentalists," in *Transnational Perspectives*, vol. 11, no. 4, 1985, pp. 20-21.

Abraham, A. J., *Islam and Christianity: Crossroads in Faith*, IN: Wyndham Hall Press, 1987.

Abraham, A. J., *Khoumani, Islamic Fundamentalists and the Contributions of Islamic Sciences to Modern Civilization*, IN: Foundations Press of Notre Dame, 1983.

Abraham, A. J., *Lebanon: A State of Siege (1975-1984)*, IN: Wyndham Hall Press, 1984.

Akhavi, Shahrough, *Religion and Politics in Contemporary Iran*, Albany: State Univ. of N.Y. Press, 1980.

Ajami, Fouad, *The Vanished Imam, Musa Sadr and the Shia of Lebanon*, N.Y.: Cornell Univ. Press, 1985.

Ali M., *The Religion of Islam*, Lahore, 1936.

Aronald, T. W., *The Preaching of Islam*, London: Constable, 1913.

Azzam, Abd al-Rahman, *The Eternal Message of Muhammad*, N.Y.: Mentor Books, 1964.

Bakhash, Shoul, *The Reign of the Ayatollahs: Iran and the Islamic Revolution*, N.Y.: Basic Books, 1984.

Capps, Walter H., (ed.), *Ways of Understanding Religion*, N.Y.: The MacMillan Co., 1972.

Deeb, Marius, *Militant Islamic Movements in Lebanon: Origins, Social Basis, and Ideology*, Center for Contemporary Arab Studies, Wash.: Georgetown Univ., 1986.

Dekmejian, R. H., *Islam in Revolution, Fundamentalism in the Arab World*, N.Y.: Syracuse Univ. Press, 1985.

Dessouki, Ali, (ed.), *Islamic Resurgence in The Arab World*, N.Y.: Preager, 1982.

El-Khawas, Mohammad, *Qaddafi, His Ideology in Theory and Practice*, VT.: Amena Books 1987.

Esposito, John L., *Islam and Politics*, Syracuse; Syracuse Univ. Press, 1984.

Esposito, John L., (ed.), *Voices of Resurgent Islam*, N.Y.: Oxford Univ. Press, 1983.

Esposito, John L., "Islam in the Politics of the Middle East," *Current History*, Feb. 1986, pp. 53-57, 81.

Farghal, Mahmoud H., "Islamic Ideology: Essence and Dimensions," *American Arab Affairs*, Spring 1983, no. 4, pp. 100-107.

Farhang, M. and Motavalli, J. H., "Iran: A Great Leap Backwards," in *The Progressive*, Aug. 1984, pp. 19-22.

Fairs, N. A., *The Arab Heritage*, N.J.: Princeton Univ. Press, 1946.

Geller, Ernest, *Moslem Society*, N.Y.: Cambridge Univ. Press, 1983.

Grunebaum, G. E., *Medieval Islam*, Ill.: Univ. of Chicago Press, 1946.

Hakim, Khalifa, *Islamic Theology*, Lahore: Pub. United Ltd., 1951.

Hallsell, Grace, *Prophacy and Politics*, N.Y.: Lawrence Hill, 1986.

Hamid, Enayat, *Modern Islamic Political Thought*, Austin.: The Univ. of Texas Press, 1982.

Hamidullah, M., *The Muslim Conduct of State*, India: Kashmiri Bazar, Lahore, 1945.

Hanafi, Hassan, "The Origins of Violence in Contemporary Islam," in *Development*, 1987, no. 1, pp. 56-61.

Hanifi, M. J., *Islam and the Transformation of Culture*, N.Y.: Asia Pub. House, 1974.

Hitti, P. K., *History of the Arabs*, N.Y.: Macmillan, 1951.

Hussain, Asaf, *Islamic Iran: Revolution and Counter-Revolution*, N.Y.: St. Martin's Press, 1985.

Keddi, N. R. and Cole, J. R. I., (ed.), *Shi'ism and Social Protest*, Conn.: Yale Univ. Press, 1986.

Kepel, Gilles, *Muslim Extremism in Egypt, The Prophet and Pharoah*, Los Angeles: Univ. of California Press, 1984.

Khomeini, A. R., *Islam and Revolution*, trans. Hamid Alger, CA.: Mizan Press, 1981.

Khomeini, A. R., *The Explanation of Problems*, CO.: Westview Press, 1984.

Khomeini, A. R., "Islamic Government," Translations on Near East and North Africa, No. 1897, *JPRS*, 72663, Jan. 1979.

Kramer, Martin, (ed.), *Shi'ism and Revolution*, CO.: Westview Press, 1987.

International Institute of Islamic Thought, *Islamization of Knowledge: General Principles and Work Plan*, VA., 1987.

Jansen, G. H., *Militant Islam*, N.Y.: Harper and Row, 1979.

Khadduri, Majid, *War and Peace in the Law of Islam*, MD.: Johns Hopkins Press, 1955.

Khalidi, Tarif, "The Idea of Progress in Classical Islam," *Journal of Near Eastern Studies*, Oct. 1981, vol. 40, no. 4, pp. 277-289.

MacDonald, D. B., *Development of Muslim Theology, Jurisprudence and Constitutional Theory*, N.Y.: Charles Scribners' Sons, 1903.

Mashiri, F., *The State and Social Revolution in Iran: A Theoretical Perspective*, N.Y.: Peter Lang, 1985.

Mortimer, Edward, *Faith and Power: The Politics of Islam*, N.Y.: Random House, 1982.

Muir, William, *The Life of Muhammad*, Edinburgh: John Grant 1912.

Nahas, Maridi, "State-System and Revolutionary Challenge: Nassar, Khoumeini, and the Middle East," *Int'l. Journal of Middle East Studies*, vol. 17, Nov. 1985, no. 4, pp. 507-527.

Nasri, Farzeen, "Iranian Studies and the Iranian Revolution," *World Politics*, vol. Xxxv, no. 4, July, 1953, pp. 607-630.

Nettler, Ronald L., "Islam vs. Israel," *Commentary*, vol. 78, no. 6, Dec. 1984, pp. 26-30.

Peters, Rudolph, *Islam and Colonialism*, N.Y.: Mouton de Gruyter, 1984.

Pipes, Daniel, *In the Path of God: Islam and Political Power*, N.Y.: Basic Books, 1983.

Pipes, Daniel, "Fundamentalist Moslems Between America and Russia," *Foreign Affairs*, Summer 1986, pp. 939-959.

Piscatori, J. P., *Islam in a World of Nation States*, Cambridge: Cambridge Univ. Press, 1986.

Rosenthal, Franz, "State and Religion According to Abu al-Hasen al-Amri," in *The Islamic Quarterly*, vol. 3, no. 1, April 1956, pp. 49-55.

Ruthven M., *Islam in the World*, N.Y.: Oxford Univ. Press, 1984.

Sardar, Ziauddin, *Islamic Futures: The Shape of Ideas to Come*, London: Mansell Pub., 1985.

Shepard, William E., "Islam and Ideology: Towards a Topology," *Int'l. Journal of Middle East Studies*, vol. 19, no. 3, August 1987.

Sivan, Emmanuel, *Radical Islam: Medieval Theology and Modern Politics*, New Haven: Yale Univ. Press, 1985.

Smith, Wilfred Cantwell, *Islam in Modern History*, N.Y.: The New American Library, 1957.

Taheri, Ammir, *Holy Terror*, N.Y.: Adler and Adler, 1987.

Tariq, Y. and Ismail, J., *Government and Politics in Islam*, N.Y.: St. Martin's Press, 1985.

Taylor, Alan R., *The Islamic Question in Middle East Politics*, Co.: Westview Press, 1988.

Taylor, Alan R., "The political Psychology of Islamic Resurgence in the Middle East," *American Arab Affairs*, Sjpring 1983, no. 4, pp. 120-131.

Tibi, Bassam, "Neo-Islamic Fundamentalism," in *Development*, 1987, no. 1, pp. 62-66.

Tritton, A. S., *The Caliphs and Their non-Moslem Subjects*, London: Oxford Univ. Press, 1930.

Voll, John O., *Islam: Continuity and Change in the Modern World*, CO.: Westview Press, 1982.

Wensinck, A. J. A., *Handbook of Early Mohammadan Tradition*, Leiden, 1927.

Wright, Robin, *Sacred Rage, The Wrath of Militant Islam*, N.Y.: Simon and Schuster, 1986.

Zonis, M. and Brumberg, D., *Khoumeini, The Islamic Republic of Iran, and the Arab World*, Mass.: Harvard Middle East Papers, (no. 5), 1987.

Zonis, Marvin, "Iran: A Theory of Revolution from Accounts of the Revolution, *World Politics*, vol. Xxxv, July 1983, no. 4, pp. 586-606.

Zonis, Marvin, "The Rule of the Clerics in the Islamic Republic of Iran," *The Annals*, vol. 482, Nov. 1985, pp. 85-108.

Zwimer, S. M., *The Law of Apostasy in Islam*, London: Marshall Bros., Ltd., 1929.

PREFACE TO PART TWO

This paper was delivered at a seminar at New York Institute of Technology during the American hostage crisis in Iran. The three-part study explores the turbulebt nature of the Islamic fundamentalist movement as it pertained, in part, to that crisis.

In the preparation of this work I have chosen to cite scholarly studies in English in the belief that the interested reader will wish to further his/her knowledge of the fundamentalist movement in Islam which is currently sweeping the lands of West Asia, the Middle East, and North Africa. Where this whirlwind of religion and emotion will terminate or if it will break against the shores of the Western World is largely undeterminable at this time. But one thing is certain, where ever it is felt, it will leave an indelible trace on east-west realationships, for some time to come.

A. J. Abraham

"Everything is not Islamic"

Dr. Rashid Habbib

PART TWO

KHOUMANI & ISLAMIC FUNDAMENTALISM:
Contributions of Islamic Sciences to Modern Civilization

A. J. Abraham
New York Institute of Technology

INTRODUCTION

This is an exploratory essay into the influence of Islamic science[1] on modern (western) civilization and the effects of Islamic fundamentalists on the nature and future of Islam. The study was prompted by the rise of Islamic militancy inaugurated by Col. Muammar al-Qadhafi's coup in Lybia (1969) and, more recently, by Ayatollah Khomeini's revolution in Iran.[2] These two revolutions, one lay and one clerical, belong to two different sects of Islam, Sunnite and Shi'ite, but they represent similar beliefs and dimensions in their reaction to western sponsored modernization; yet it has been Khomeini who has articulated those views more clearly in recent times.

In the name of Islamic reform, the Moslem fundamentalists seek to purify their societies from the process of modernization (westernization) under the guise of eliminating the traces of "neo-colonialism," "neo-imperialism," and, the old stand-by, "Zionism." In essence, they believe that westernization in the form of modern democracy, socialism, and secular law are contrary to Islamic traditions and, hence, they wish to eliminate them where ever they exist, in order to return to a pristine Islam via "Revolutions in Reverse."

The fundamentalists are not against modern science, technology, armaments or bureaucratic administration[3] but, rather, they oppose all social or cultural changes that modernization creates. At first glance the old division between Islamic science and foreign science prevails, although the scientific methodology of modern times can affect both almost equally. Thus, in recent times, this separation has been seen as false and hypocritical by some Moslem intellectuals, as science and culture become increasingly interrelated in the non-western world.

Scientific methodology not withstanding, Islam's fundamentalists believe that the only acceptable ideology is Islam, all others are at best only partially valid for the Quran, the Holy Book of Islam, represents the only totally valid statement of life and world order. Therefore, no adaption of Moslem institutions or laws to foreign systems is possible and, certaily, no conversion of life styles from those set in the Quran can be tolerated.[4] Before the end of time, these fundamentalists are confident, all ideologies will perish or be transformed into the Islamic model; hence, western styled democracy, socialism and secular law will have ebbed away or be violently thrown upon the trash heap of civilizations already demised. Consequently, man's human constructs and ideas are deemed inferior to Allah's (God's) decrees, as interpreted by the Moslem fundamentalists.

What the Islamic fundamentalists have failed to observe is that modern democracy, socialism and secular law are, in part, a by-product of the Islamic sciences, transmitted to the West as a consequence of the Arab presence in Spain and Italy in the Middle Ages, and that these ideas differ today from the past as a result of intellectual evolution in the modern world.

§ § §

NOTES

1. The "Islamic sciences"" include all materials that specifically regard the religion of Islam such as the Quran, hadith (Muhammad's speech), sirat (Muhammad's biography), shari'a (Islamic law), tafsir (exegesis), kalam (thelogy) and the Arabic language. The "foreign sciences" include mathematics, medicine, history, geography, philosophy and the physical sciences which lie outside the relm of religion. Due to the limitations of space in this study, we shall restrict ourselves to the Quran for it is unquestionably accepted by all Moslems. On the Quran's composition see, P. K. Hitti, *History of the Arabs*, 10 ed., New York: St. Martin's Press, 1970, pp. 123-127; Maurice Gaudefroy-Demombynes, *Muslim Institutions*, (trans. By John P. Macgregor), London: Bradford and Dickens, 1950, pp. 61-65. It should be noted that the Earthly Quran was compiled in eight segments which separated the religious chapters revealed in Mecca from the administrative chapters revealed in Medinah, but, later, they were combined into four separate yet complete books unifying church and state. During the reign of the Caliph Uthman (644-656 A.DJ.), the Medinah codex was "canonized" and the other three Qurans were destroyed to resolve differences in text. (Uthman's opposition accused him of tampering with the text of the Quran and destroying the others to eliminate the evidence against him, but he may have acted to prevent varying interpretations and emphasis from arising in Islam, a charge levelled by Moslems at the four Gospels of Christianity.) The final text of the Quran was completed in 933 A.D. when diacritical marks were added

to the text to standardize readings. However, this author attests to the uncreatedness of the Quran, the Earthly Quran being a true copy of the preserved Quran in God's (Allah's) possession.

2. The rise of Islamic militancy is, in part, visible in the recent Lebanese "civil war," and in the activities of the Moro Liberation Front in the Philippines. Hindu-Moslem tensions are on the increase in the Indian subcontinent, once again.

3. Moslem fundamentalists, for the most part, are against the changes in culture and lifestyle that modernization creates. To say that they are against all modernization is a prevalent misconception in the western media.

4. Malachi Martin, *The Encounter*, New York: Farrar, Straus and Giroux, 1969, p. 390.

CHAPTER EIGHT

TRANSLATION AND TRANSITION

Approximately one hundred years after the death of the Prophet Muhammad, the Arab armies had destroyed the remnants of the Byzantine and Persian empires and expanded their power to the fringes of China and the vital limbs of Europe. In perhaps the most potent form of religious, cultural and linguistic imperialism that can be recalled, the Arabs conquered those peoples and assimilated their intellectual heritage. In time, they became great innovators and scholars, thereby contributing vastly to all who came under their sway. Yet the Arabs were not loved for heavy handed tactics were employed in the hopes of gaining uniformity in faith and culture. The Persians (Iranians) resented domination by the Arabs[1] and, thus, they generated a number Islamic heresies and Prophets of their own.[2] In North Africa, the Berbers were to find Prophets of their own who received revealed Qurans in their language.[3] Consequently, sectarian strains and political-religious fragmentation coupled to external assaults terminated the proud and mighty Arab empire. But the political end did not signal the eclipse of Arab intellectual brilliance for the corpus of their literary works were to live on in Europe where Moslem East and Christian West were bridged.

Islamic Spain (711-1492 A.D.) and Moslem Italy under the Aghlibids (800-909 A.D.) and the Fatimids (909-1171 A.D.) flourished intellectually at the many centers of learning founded by the Arabs and, eventually, the fruits of that learning helped to initiate the European Renaissance. The Christian reconquest of Spain, in particular, took advantage of the ethnic, racial and cultural rift that had developed between the Hellenized and sophisticated Arabs and the intolerant Berber fundamentalists, the Almoravids (1056-1147 A.D.) and the Almohads (1130-1269 A.D.), who had recently invaded the peninsula as allies of their co-religionists. The cultural harmony and cordiality that had once emerged between Christian and Moslem in parts of Spain vanished in the wake of the newcomers,[4] while the rising tide of European opinion saw the continued presence of the Moslems in Europe as a threat to the evolving feudal system and the Christian kingdoms of Spain and Italy.

The ensuing Moslem-Christian conflict was political in an attempt to end the Arab domination over parts of Europe most importantly in Spain where Islam's tenure had lasted centuries. However, by December 1492, the political reconquest of Spain was completed when the last Arab amirate in Granada (the Nasrids of the Banu Ahmar, 1230-1492 A.D.) surrendered to the Christian forces.[5] But Islamic society remained a fact of life. Contrary to popular myth and misconception, the Moslems were not evicted; they were too numerous and too important an economic element to be lost.[6] In time, a significant number of Moslems did leave Spain for North Africa and lands east, but the overwhelming majority remained free to practice their faith and culture.

In 1569, a revolt of the Spanish Moslems was instigated from Algiers which resulted in the eviction of some of its participants.[7] That revolt changed the attitudes of many of the Christian kings and clergy and, soon afterwards, edicts of expulsion were issued. For the most part the edicts were not applied or enforced since they were designed to prevent further interference in Spanish affairs by the Ottoman governor of Algiers. In the meantime, the Christian clergy of Spain began to take an initiative to convert or win the Arab and Spanish Moslems to the Catholic faith, without insulting the beliefs of either religion.[8] The initial stage of that effort, however, can be traced back to the ninth century.

A group of Christians known as the martyrs of Cordova had launched a separate movement designed to challenge Moslem beliefs and openly defend their faith in the face of powerful Islamic authorities; the result of their efforts brought flogging and death to its participants.[9] But, the movement gained momentum as additional martyrs publically denounced the Prophet Muhammad resulting in their swift public executions.[10] The whole process was a monumental failure for no converts were obtained from Islam. It should be noted that the polemics used by the martyr's clique was of poor quality for they lacked accurate knowledge of Islam often misinterpreting the faith.[11]

Over the next two centuries a change of tactics resulted emphasizing Christology and, particularly, the unity and Trinity of God.[12] The approach seemed to reject the revelations of the Quran being contrary to its implications. Thus, this new tactic, preaching the Gospels to the Moslems, was the second monumental failure of the Christian effort to convert Moslems to Christianity.

By the eleventh century, the Christian leadership began to take a serious look into the Islamic sciences. The earliest translation of the Quran into a western language was inaugurated by Peter the Venerable, the Abbot of Cluny, in 1142 A.D., while he was on a visit to Castile. But it was Mark of Toledo who gave the Christian clergy the first extremely accurate view of the Quran, in the thirteenth century.[13] Thus, after centuries of failure, the Christian church had to come to terms with the divine revelations of both the Gospels and the Quran. The ideological convulsions which began once again were centered upon the major intellectual order of the Catholic church, the Dominicans.[14]

The Dominican order was founded in the thirteenth century by Saint Dominic of Castile who was well versed in the concepts and views of both Christianity and Islam.[15] Ramon Marti, a member of that order, was the first to challenge the beliefs of Islam based upon the translation of the Quran and some of the Islamic sciences. His major work entitled *Fourfold Condemnation*[16] was a polemic against Quranic interpretations, however, it gained no meaningful results. Yet, his efforts encouraged other scholars with a broad based and accurate knowledge of Islamics to work with the Quran and the Gospels. Hence, Dominican strategy shifted in the late thirteenth century to one of embellishing arguments well known to the Christian Arabs of the Near East, particularly the Maronite Catholic Church of Lebanon. (That church had established contacts with Rome for centuries.) The Dominicans, therefore, sought to harmonize the conflicting passages of the Quran and the Gospels regarding the nature of Christ and His death by crucifixion.[17] The differences between Christian revelation and Moslem revelation was approached as controversies of interpretation rather than substance, thus facilitating the conversion of the majority of Europe's Moslems to the Christian faith, in time. What is, however, of greater importance is that European scholars could approach the Islamic sciences in confidence, free from the fear of being "misled" from their beliefs. Eventually, the theological implications inherent in Islamics lost their prominence as Spain and Italy became almost completely Catholic. But, the socio-economic ideas to be found in the Quran and other Islamic works, especially those concerning democratic, social and legal precepts, were in part incorporated into the Western intellectual tradition. This legacy lived on through the Middle Ages to influence modern democracy, socialism and secular law.

NOTES

1. The Persians (Iranians) believe that they are superior to the Arabians and resented conquest by foreigners. The other peoples of the fertile crescent, however, were under Byzantine rule and, consequently, saw the Arabian advance as a liberation of sorts.

2. Al-Muqanna, the Veiled Prophet of Khurasan, posed as the incarnation of God defying the Abbasid Caliph, al-Mahdi, for several years. His following was extensive and his organization powerful. This raises an issue in the concept of prophethood in Islam, for why should so many Moslems support al-Muqanna and other Moslems who claimed to be prophets if it is clear that the Prophet Muhammad is the seal of all prophets, presenting mankind with God's final, complete and perfected revelation. Most historians of the period ascribe Muqanna's extensive support to his pious character, to the fact that there is no separation of church and state in Islam, or to the widely based social discontent among the newly converted Moslems or to some sort of ethno-national factor. Those facts clearly explain the rise of opposition to the non-Shi'ite Caliphate but not necessarily the acceptance of "new" prophets. Muhammad, the messenger of God, was clearly the last true prophet of the Arabian community but the non-Arabian Moslems may not have foreclosed the door of prophacy. Apparantly, some Moslems may have interpreted the word "seal" to mean "symbol" rather than the last one. Therefore, al-Muqanna and others may have been seen as minor prophets sent by God to retain Islam's purity and to end the usurper Caliphate. As long as they opperated within the Islamic context, not establishing separate religions not akin to Islam, they found strong support among the Moslem community. Had these prophets been charlatans they would have been easily discredited and would have never gained a large following. (Although defeated militarily, they succeeded in influencing Islamic ideas, in a limited way.)

3. A Berber Quran consisting of eighty chapters was revealed to Salih al-Muminin (al-Mu'min) of the Bergawata tribe (approx. 744 A.D.), in North Africa. He also claimed to be the expected Mahdi of Islam. After his death, the movement continued under his grandson, Yunis. In the Rif region of northern Morraco, another Berber named Hamim proclaimed a revealed Quran. He died fighting the Umayyids of Spain

in 927 A.D.. See: Charles-Andre Julien, *History of North Africa*, New York: Praeger, 1970, p. 33. (From the orthodox point of view, these Qurans are considered medieval forgeries. Christianity also considers a number of ancient Gospels apocryphal.)

4. For a brief and scholarly study of Islamic Spain see: W. Montgomery Watt, *A History of Islamic Spain*, Edinburgh University Press, 1965.

5. Watt, *op. cit.*, pp. 147-150.

6. Robert I. Burns, S.J., "Christian-Islamic Confrontation in the West: The Thirteenth Century Dream of Conversion," *The American Historical Review*, vol. 76, no. 2, Dec. 1971, pp. 1386-1434.

7. Watt, *op. cit.*, p. 154.

8. Burns, *op. cit.*, p. 1389.

9. Norman Daniel, *The Arab and Mediaeval Europe*, London: Longmans Group Ltd., 1975, pp. 23-24. The leading figures were Perfectus (al-Kamil), John (Yahya/Yuhanna) and Isacc (Ishaq). On the nature of Christian and Moslem martyrdom see: Wilfred C. Smith, *Islam in Modern History*, New York: The New American Library, 1957, p. 37 (f.n. 27).

10. Daniel, *op, cit.*, p. 38.

11. *Ibid.*, pp. 40-41.

12. *Ibid.*, p. 81. The Trinity of Christianity has been and often continues to be misunderstood by Moslems. At first, some Moslems believed that the Trinity consisted of Mary, Jesus and God. This heresy, apparantly, originated among the ancient Collridians and with the Borborians of Armenia. The second misconception, that Christians believe in three gods (tri-theism), can be traced back to the pagans of Arabia who sought to play off the Prophet Muhammad's Christian supporters against the Moslem community which knew little of Christian beliefs. This ploy, had it been successful, would have enabled the pagans to accuse Muhammad of hypocracy-supporting some polytheists while opposing others. The pagans were frustrated, however, when God interceded

with a revelation (Q 1V: 171) instructing the Christians not to say that God is three.

For Christianity, the Trinity represents three physical manifestations of God intersecting with mankind at different times without compromising His composite unity. (Perhaps the best scientific explanation of the Trinity comes from the study of change of state in modern physics whereby the physical properties of a substance can appear differently and follow different laws of existence without diminishing its unity, energy or matter.) Since the God of Judaism, Christianity and Islam is a living God (not virtual or imaginary), the Trinity is described as persons. Furthermore, Jesus clarifies his relationship to God in essence and nature by stating "I and the Father are One" (Jn: 10: 30-33) and He claimed to be the "resurrection and the life" (Jn: II: 25-27) a statement understood by some of His contemporaries to contain the two properties that belong solely to God. Jesus, also, claimed to exist prior to the Prophet Abraham (Jn: 8-58). His sonship was revealed to the Apostles at the Transfiguration when God's voice was heared to say, "This is my Son, the Beloved, Listen to Him," (Mk: 27: 43). Thus, even when heresies existed among the Christians of Arabia, it is doubtful that they could have misrepresented the Trinity to the extent of polytheism. The Moslems of Arabia accused the Christians of unbelief (kufr) rather than idolatry or polytheism (shirk). For more on this see: W. Montgomery Watt, *Islam and the Integration of Society*, Gt. Britain: Northwetern University Press, 1961, p. 267. (Lastly, and perhaps most importantly, God refers to Himself in the Quran in the third person plural.)

There is a far more plausible explanation for the revelation instructing Christians not to say that God is three. At one point, while the Prophet Muhammad was reciting chapter LIII of the Quran, Satan, the evil force, put into the Prophet's mind a few words of praise for *three* goddessed of the Arabian polytheists (al-Lat, al-Uzza and Manat) which the pagans, later, presented to the Christians of Arabia as an arrangement for reconciliation between themselves and the Moslems. Since the Christians might have accepted those three godesses as part of an Islamic "trinity" of sorts, the Lord, apparantly, issued forth his command not to say the God is three.

13. Daniel, *op. cit.*, pp. 230-231.

14. *Ibid.*, pp. 254-255.

15. The Dominicans are best known for their work combatting Christian heresies in Europe and for their intellectual endeavors.

16. Daniel, *op. cit.*, p. 239.

17. During the lifetime of the Prophet Muhammad, the Christians of Arabia lived in safety but they paid a small poll tax for their protection. If the Islamic state could not protect them, the tax was to be returned, however, it later symbolized the superiority of the Moslems and the subjugation of the Christians.

It was not until the Caliphate of Omar (634-644 A.D.) that problems between Moslems and Christians occured and the first attempt to "harmonize" the conflicting passages of the Quran and the Gospels took place. When the Christians stopped paying the poll tax claiming that they, like the Moslems, submitted to the will of God and recognized Muhammad as a true Prophet for the Moslems, Omar, then, objected to the Divinity of Jesus. The Christians, even when accepting Islamic profession of faith, refused to deny the Divinity of Jesus-His spiritual nature. They argued that restricting the role of Jesus to that of only a prophet was an error and, then, they proceeded to support their views by citing passages from the Quran in defense of their faith.

Briefly, on the nature of Jesus, the Eastern Christians, particularly the Maronites of Lebanon, interpreted chapter II: 87, 253 and chapter V: 113 of the Quran regarding the strengthening/supporting of Jesus by the Holy Spirit (the Third Person of the Trinity) as an indication of His divine spirit and essence. Moslems interpret the Holy Spirit to be Gabriel, the angel of revelation. On His miracles, the Christians maintained that God permitted Jesus to work miracles so that a unity of volition would prevail between them, but that Jesus affected them through His own power. The Moslem scholars interpreted "permission" to imply that God is the author and power behind the miracles of Jesus, thus making Jesus a powerless man.

The greatest controversy ensued over the death and crucifixion of Jesus. The Quran states (chapter IV: 157) that "they slew him not nor crucified him, but it appeared so unto them." Docetic Christology, then prevalent in the Hellenistic Near East, Maintained that the Lord (Jesus) was man in appearance only and that He *appeared* only to suffer and die. Thus, the Eastern Arab Christians interpreted the first part of the Quranic phrase to reflect that thinking. Nevertheless, the Christians maintained that God's spriitual nature was encompassed in the body of Jesus, and that body suffered death by crucifixion but was restored at the resurrection, hence His death was temporary. Thus, the first part of chapter IV: 157 of the Quran supported the resurrection of Jesus, in Christian eyes. Centuries after the Quran was completed, Moslem intellectuals claimed that the "appearance" referred to in that chapter of the Quran resulted from a substitution being made for Jesus at the time of His execution by Simon the Cyrene (an idea originally put forth by a Gnostic named Basilides; it, later, gained some circulation in the *Heresies Answered* of Irenaeus.) In more modern times, Moslem psychologists favor the idea that God created the illusion of crucifixion in the minds of the enemies of Jesus.

There is also much in the way of agreement in Islam and Christianity. Chapter IV: 171 of the Quran says "Jesus the Messiah, the son of Mary, was a Messenger of God, His Word which He placed in Mary, and His Spirit." Consequently, the Quran accepts the Virgin birth of Jesus.

Perhaps because of these exchanges of opinion which ensued for centuries, Moslems were eventually discouraged from questioning Christians and Jews regarding their faiths and from attempting any critical analysis of the Quran. In time, the fundamentalist theologian Abd Allah al-Baydawi put forth the claim that the Christian scriptures were corrupted or, at best, the Christians had corrupted their meaning. Finally, the Gospels were given extremely limited validity. (That which is valid in the Gospels is only what agreed with the then current interpretations of the Quran.) To date, however, no evidence of corruption has been authenticated, but, perhaps, Christian interpretations of the Gospels have become synonymous with corruption for the Islamic fundamentalists.

On Docetic Christology see: Charles Guignebert, *The Early History of Christiantiy*, New York: Twayne Pub., 1927, pp. 146-147; Gustav Von Grunebaum, *Modern Islam*, New York: Alfred A. Knopf, Inc., 1964, p. 8. For the opposing view, the inability to harmonize Christianity and Islam, see: Smith, *op. cit.*, p. 25 (fn. 13). On Moslem attitudes regarding the Bible see: W. Montgomery Watt, *Islam and the Intergation of Society*, pp. 258-276.

CHAPTER NINE

THE ISLAMIC IDEAL AND THE MODERN WORLD

The three major aspects of modern society most strongly opposed by the Moslem fundamentalists are the western institutuions of democracy, socialism and secular law which they see as foreign and unacceptable intrusions into the political body of Islam. These ideas and institutions have, however, at least one set of roots in the Quran and in the precedents to be found in the life of the Prophet Muhammad.[1] No doubt, those concepts and institutions have evolved in the course of time into present-day patterns that the restricted learning of the Islamic fundamentalists may not recognize, but, clearly they are not alien to Islamic traditions.

The rudimentary concepts of democracy, socialism and secular law, in part, entered the intellectual realm of the western world through translations of Arabic works found in the great libraries of Islamic Spain and Italy. For those scholars of Islam no separation of church and state existed hence, theory and practice converged only later being separated after the reconquest of those areas by the Christian kingdoms. Consequently, Europe and the Moslem world diverged for centuries, reconverging in the twentieth century when the West dominated the Middle East and some of the other lands of Islam. That short period of tutelage lasted for the interwar years (1914-1945), during which westernization was stressed.

When Europe left the Middle East and other parts of West Asia in the post World War II period, a reaction set in under the leadership of Islamic fundamentalists who particularly resented and opposed the trend towards separation of church and state. Today, the fundamentalists are on the upswing once again, and the success of Imam Khomeini has focused their thoughts and opinions in a highly sophisticated and articulated manner.[2]

Originally an address on Islamic jurisprudence given to theology students entitled *Governance of Jurisprudent*, Khomeini presents the views of fundamentalist Islam regarding the role of the clergy in the Moslem states. He supports his opinions by citing vernerable Shi'ite elites of the past as well as references to the Quran and Hadiths relying on those interpretations that suit his convictions. Included in his analysis is a scathing denounciation of American and British influences and ideas, foreigners, and Jewish,

Christian and Baha'i missions, all of which represent "sick ideas" to a Moslem state and are of no true consequence.[3] Without insight into the benefits of modern thought and cultures or the temperance of a pluralistic society, Khomeini sees all divergence of belief and speculation as a threat to Islamic unity and clerical power. Yet, he admits the benefits and desirability of modern science and technology, maintaining the dichotomy of Islamic science and foreign science prevalent in Classical Islamic civilization.[4] Thus, Ayatollah Khomeini presented the view of an Islamic state controlled by an authoritative clergy who rule it from above in the name of God.[5] The citizen has only duties and obligations to the state, and unlike the democracies of the West, the Islamic parliament administers the laws and decrees of the clergy but has no legislative powers on behalf of its constituents.[6] The individual exists to serve the state and its religious elites. Khomeini presents his arguments in an elucidative and uncompromisingly positive manner, but his interpretations and conclusions present only one panorama of Islamic society and culture, past, present and future.

From another perspective it can be shown that the ideas and institutions condemned by the Islamic fundamentalists were embodied in the Islamic community, from its genesis.

The Islamic community represents the essence of a democratic idea but unlike democracy in the West, it functioned with little assistance from a professional class of politicians,[7] who were not needed for rudimentary democratic proceedings. Allegience is to God above all and, hence, in accordance with the Prophet's belief, the members of the Moslem community are "as equal as the teeth of a comb,"[8] a fundamental implication of the western world's concept of universal manhood suffrage. (It should be noted that Christianity maintains the belief in the absolute equality of all mankind.) In consultations, no group in the Islamic society is to have authority over another, so that majority rule is upheld. Thus, consultation with the community is a basic political rule giving the citizen a say in his destiny.[9] (Even the clergy has no right to violate, modify or abrogate this command from God.) If an elected official appears to be dictatorial or abusive, the citizenry can remove the leadership unless reforms are enacted.[10] This concept implies the modern system of political recall.

The Islamic community in its embroyonic form represents direct democracy similar to the democracy of ancient Greece, both of which have limitations that make some of their concepts obsolete in the modern world. They represent, however, truly democratic ideas which can be modified for today's complex society. Those political thoughts set the stage for Islam's social life.

Social liberalism and human justice for Moslems are implicit in the classical Islamic state. The social structure of Islam drew its inspiration from the Quran whose numerous citations established a leveling effect within the Moslem community, providing for a degree of security in an age of uncertainty and instability. Aid to the less fortunate and condemnation of exploitation[11] created a socialistic atmosphere. Like Judaism and Christianity, Islam presents a moral and ethical world view in which the administration strives for a higher standard of living for its citizens within limited economic and social stratification.[12] The state may redistribute income for the benefit of the people while private property is to be regulated to avoid public exploitation.[13] The system provided a degree of social security enforced by law.

The Islamic state exists to execute Islamic law, the Shari'ah often called "God's Law" by Moslems.[14] Four schools of law, the Shafi'ite, the Hanafite, the Malikite and the Hanbalite evolved for the Sunnite branch of Islam while three schools of law, the Jafari, the Ismaili and the Zaydi, grew out of the Shi'ite branch of the faith. The origins of Islamic jurisprudence (usul al-fiqh) are derived from the Quran, the Sunna (precedents) set by the Prophet Muhammad, ijma (consensus) of the Moslem community, and qiyas (analogy), a form of analyitical reasoning involving Quranic text.[15] (Qiyas is at least in part elicited from the Quran by the process of human reasoning.)[16] The human factor gives qiyas a secular function and the process itself is inductive rather than diductive so that its conclusions results in only a hypothetical probability of validity. Consensus of the community, however, allows for a virtual garden of human interpretations involving intellectual intercourse.[17]

These sources of law did not suffice in many cases for unchartered areas and problems were bound to arise as Islam expanded into a major world religion. When no valid interpretation could be drawn from previous sources, the Islamic judges added a fifth source of law called ra'y/ijtihad (personal opinion).[18] At first, personal opinion was criticized for resulting in "remote conclusions which are based neither on the Koran nor on sunna, are acceptable to no one except their author...."[19] It is purely secular[20] but has been accepted and has remained in operation in the Islamic world for centuries.

The Prophet Muhammad, also, allowed for the unwritten local customs and secular pre-Islamic practices known as urf/ada/ amal to exist along side the nascent Shari'ah. Those practices that were not directly prohibited by the Quran or by Muhammad's discourse were to remain in force[21] as well as new concepts that entered the Moslem world in the course of military expansion. Apparently, the Prophet saw no dilemma between secular and religious sources of law for his community, as long as morality was upheld. In a discourse recorded in the heresiographical work of the Asharite mutakallim (theologian), Abu al-Fath al-Shahrastani entitled *Kitab al-Milal wa al-Nihal* (The Book of Creeds (Religions) and Sects), the Prophet Muhammad and his appointed qadi (judge) for al-Yamin, Mu'adh ibn Jabal, exchanged the following views:

"Muhammad: How wilt thou decide when a question arises?
Mu'adh: According to The Book of Allah.
Muhammad: And if thou findest naught therin?
Mu'adh: According to the sunnah of the Messenger of Allah.
Muhammad: And if thou findest naught therin?
Mu'adh: Then I shall follow (apply) my own reasoning (opinion)."[22]

Thus, we can ascertain that for the Prophet Muhammad the secular and the divine were not in total conflict but, rather, they were alternate forms of jurisprudence for the Moslem community in order to compliment the evolution of justice. Apparently, the Prophet, in his divinely inspired wisdom, forsaw the impossibility of employing the Quran and his discourse (the Hadiths) to all future situations.

Moslem jurists often characterize Islamic law as "scientific law" claiming that its validity is as universal as the laws of natural and physical science. Yet, it should be understood that even the most rigorous scientific laws are subject to abrogation, revision, reinterpretation and modification within mans knowledge and experience. Scientific or not, all legal systems, religious or secular, exhibit similar tensions resulting from human interaction and the reasoning of the jurists. We have discussed, up to this point, the evolution of the Islamic schools of legal thought[23] and the underlying tensions between divine revelations and human reasoning,[24] in a legal context. We must now add to them the strains created between liberal and conservative interpretations of the Quran and the Shari'ah,[25] as well as the clash of doctrine opposed by practical reality.[26] No legal system can be free from tension but in Islamic law tensity seems to stem mostly from attempting to fit all conditions of life into a fixed set of patterns that govern and regulate the relations of Moslems to one another and to non-Moslems for all times, places, human conditions and situations. Regulation is enforced by severe punishment including mutilation of the non-conformist, and often that creates new conflicts between the policy of the government and the interpretations of the religious leadership. This conditions produces an unstable status for religious minorities in the Moslem world, particularly for non-Moslems.

In the Middle Ages, Christian and Jewish subjects in the Moslem kingdoms were called dhimmis (people of the Covenant) and they were treated differently depending on the ruler's policy and the school of Islamic law to which they were subjected,[27] but, on the whole, they were generally tolerated. All other groups were treated as the enemies of Islam to face eventual conversion or extinction, unless granted immunity by the Quran. Today, the polytheists enemies of the Prophet have disappeared in the Moslem world leaving the Christians, the Jews, and the Zororastrians (called Ahl al-Kitab) as the "sole representitives of infidelity" in the Middle East, along side Moslem minorities.[28] Of all the Christian sects in the Arab east, only the Maronites of Lebanon found refuge from dhimmi status in their mountain highlands and, consequently, their patriarch was invested by Rome.[29] Those factors freed them from Moslem domination and the restrictions that the other minorities could not avoid, hence, the Maronite community flourished in an atmosphere of freedom and humanitarianism. (This factor, although often denied in the Lebanese civil war, remains a strong psychological undercurrent for the Christian community in Lebanon.)

Regarding the other minorities in medieval Islam, they were subject to their own religious laws regarding personal status; but they were seen as inferior beings in the eyes of the Islamic clergy and the Shari'ah. They suffered limitations in their status as citizens; their legal testimony was often not accepted or taken very lightly.[30] In addition, the dhimmi had to pay a special poll tax, and they were not allowed to ride horses, carry arms or serve in the army. They were distinguished from the Moslems by dress and their houses and religious institutions could not be taller than those of the Moslems. New churches could not be built and old ones could not be repaired, many were destroyed in time. Christian religious observances and processions had to be moderate, of low profile, when permitted, and the ringing of church bells was to be muted. In *Kitab al-Kharaj* (The Book of Land Tax), Abu Yusuf, an eight century scholar, informs us that Babtism was forbidden at times. And, in some Moslem states, the use of wine for the sacrifice of the Mass was outlawed, under Islamic law.

On the personal level, dhimmis could not marry Moslem women for wives are the property of their husbands, in Islam. Moslem men, however, may wed dhimmi women upon the condition that they publicaly adherer to Islam and raise their children as Moslems. In time, Islamic law became an extremely potent instrument for the conversion of the non-Moslems to Islam since it was the only means by which they could avoid "constant and intensive humiliation."

Islamic law also provided some unique problems for Moslems when administered by fundamentalist judges. Moslem women lacked equal rights under Islamic law, hence, they suffered from discriminatory legislation on a private level in regard to marriage rules, divorce, inheritance, visitation rights for children of divorced parents, and in regard to their chastity, fidelity and personal freedom.[31] The testimony of women, in the eyes of the judiciary, is worth one-half the testimony of a man - the basic value of a Moslem women when compared to a Moslem man.

For these reasons, Islamic law has been criticized as discriminatory for pronouncing judgements that are not based on concepts of equality or purely on the basis of the evidence. The legal system lacks a due process arrangement and a jury of ones peers to evaluate evidence. Yet, it should be understood as a system that reflected the Middle Ages and one which gave Moslems a degree of security in an age of insecurity and, in some cases, it protected the non-Moslem from arbitrary abuse by traditionalists and other zealots who would have liked to see them forcibly converted to Islam. Clearly, the idea of legal limitations on the prerogatives of a judge or ruler in the western world seem to have been influenced, to some degree, by the implied limitations in the administration of Moslem law to non-Moslems, through contacts with Islamic Spain. (Roman Law should not be discounted as a factor in the evolution of legal limitations, but for all practical purposes, Roman law was eclipsed by Islamic law in Spain, for centuries.) The *History of The Judges of Cordova* written by al-Khushani, a Malikite jurist, supports the view that legal limitations were in effect during his stay in Spain.

As far as the Islamic fundamentlists are concerned, however, a person's legal and human rights are what the Quran says they are, particularly regarding the status of non-Moslems and, therefore, no advancements towards equal rights between Moslems and non-Moslems are possible. Consequently, most of the Moslem states have istituted secular law in recent times to balance the Islamic legal authorities. The fundamentalists and their allies do not perceive the secular initiatives as advances in justice but, rather, as foreign imports to be eradicated. The implementation of non-Moslem law codes are regarded as legal trickery (hiyal) established by secular political parties to provide socially desirable changes in the status of the citizenery at home and in the eyes of the world.[32]

Even in the world arena, the civil law of nations, the UN Charter, the international (UN sponsored) declaration of human rights are invalid[33] for Islam's fundamentalists because no provision for them exists in the Quran or the Shari'ah. And, within the Middle East and the Islamic world at large, both Israel and Lebanon are viewed as part of the outside world to which the Islamic fundamentalists are irrevocably hostile, and with which no concession can be made, no acceptable arrangement can be permitted until they become Moslem in character, administration and law.[34] Hence, Khomeini's shift in policy against Israel and Col. Qadhafi's efforts in Lebanon can be understood from the fundamentalists point of view. Furthermore, the Arab and Moslem attitude towards Israel is based upon the issue of the rights of the Palestinian people regarding their struggle for sovereignity in their homeland (Palestine/Israel). In the case of Lebanon, the fundamentalists see Christian Lebanon, with its emphasis on equal rights for both the Christian and Moslem communities, as a spiritual, intellectual and military failure. (Of all the Arab states, Lebanon alone has maintained a dual character, Christian and Moslem.)

This overview of secular law and Islamic law should confirm the belief that neither system of jurisprudence can produce complete peace of mind, justice or human happiness for it is the nature of man that produces physical and psychological problems in human relations. But, if a combination of both legal traditions can increase the level of justice while advancing secular and liberal human rights, then implementation of non-Islamic legal systems may not be contrary to the spirit of Islam.

NOTES

1. Space does not allow for a full analysis of the role of all the Islamic sciences in the evolution of democracy, socialism and law.

2. Ayatollah R. Khomeyni, "Islamic Government," *Translations on Near East and North Africa*, no. 1897, JPRS, 72663, Jan. 1979. For the Sunnite point of view see: Al-Qathafi, Muammar, *The Green Book*, part 1, *The Solution of the Problem of Democcracy*, "*The Authority of the People*;" part 2, *The Solution of the Economic Problem*, "*Socialism;*" and part 3, *The Social Basis of the Third Universal Theory*, Tripoli, Libya.

3. Khoumani, *op. cit.*, pp. 4, 6-9, 57-58, 63-64, 67.

4. *Ibid.*, p. 64.

5. *Ibid.*, pp. 7, 9, 17, 19, 22, 32, 37, 41-42.

6. *Ibid.*, pp. 7, 9, 17, 20-21, 37, 41-42.

7. Abdel Moghny Said, *Arab Socialism*, Gt. Britain: Blandford Press, Ltd., 1972, p. 46; Stephen Goode, *The Prophet and the Revolutionary*, New York: Franklin Watts, Inc., 1975, p. 20.

8. Said, *op, cit.*, pp. 46-47.

9. Quran 88; 22.

10. Said, *op. cit.*, pp. 25-27, 48; Quran 9: 34.

11. Said, *op. cit.*, p. 24.

12. *Ibid.*, p. 25; Quran 53: 38-41, Quran 59: 7.

13. *Ibid.*, p. 28.

14. Strictly speaking, God's law can not be applied on Earth unless God is the sole judge and jury in each and every case, so that contamination by

human thought is impossible. H. A. R. Gibb and Harold Bowen, *Islamic Society and the West*, vol. I, part II, London: Oxford University Press, 1957, p. 115.

15. Joseph Schacht, *The Origins of Islamic Jurisprudence*, London: Oxford University Press, 1959, p. 135; Gaudefroy-Demombynes, *op. cit.*, pp. 61-69; Gustav Von Grunebaum, *Medieval Islam*, Chicago: University of Chicago Press, 1953, pp. 142-153; Majid Khadduri, *Islamic Jurisprudence, Shafi'is Risala*, Baltimore: The Johns Hopkins Press, 1961.

16. Reuben Levy, *The Social Structure of Islam*, London: Cambridge University Press, 1969, pp. 165-167; Von Grunebaum, *Modern Islam*, p. 28.

17. Levy, *op, cit.*, pp. 168-169.

18. Schacht, *op. cit.*, pp. 98-99; Gaudefroy-Demombynes, *op, cit.*, p. 66.

19. Schacht, *op. cit.*, p. 102.

20. *Ibid.*, p. 129.

21. Levy, *op. cit.*, pp. 248-249.

22. Hitti, *op. cit.*, p. 397; Von Grunebaum, *Medieval Islam*, p. 147; Reynold A. Nicholson, *A Literary History of the Arabs*, Cambridge: At The University Press, 1969, p. 341; F. E. Peters, *Allah's Commonwealth*, New York: Simon and Schuster, 1973, pp. 701-702.

23. Noel J. Coulson, *Conflicts and Tensions in Islamic Jurisprudence*, Chicago: The University of Chicago Press, 1969, pp. 21-24.

24. *Ibid.*, pp. 3-7.

25. *Ibid.*, pp. 40-57.

26. *Ibid.*, pp. 58-76.

27. Gibb and Bowen, *op. cit.*, p. 207.

28. *Ibid.*, p. 208.

29. *Ibid.*, pp. 230, 248.

30. On the status and restrictions of the dhimmis see: Hitti, *op. cit.*, pp. 252-359; Gibb and Bowen, *op, cit.*, pp. 208, 258; Levy, *op. cit.*, pp. 66-67; Von Grunebaum, *Medieval Islam*, pp. 177-185.

31. Levy, *op. cit.*, pp. 94, 97, 113-116, 119, 121-124, 139, 145; Gaudefroy-Demombynes, *op. cit.*, p. 132; Quran 2: 228.

32. Coulson, *op. cit.*, pp. 90-91.

33. Martin, *op. cit.*, p. 393.

34. *Ibid.*, p. 395.

CHAPTER TEN

TENSIONS AND RESOLUTIONS FOR THE FUTURE

Many scholars of Islam have tried to explain the "backward" nature of Islamic society by insisting that the true difference between Islamic society and the West lies in the belief that Islam unlike Christianity, is a way of life that permeated the Moslems from the cradel to the grave.[1] By implication, that statement is insulting to Christianity for it asserts that the Christian faith is not a way of life, or at least less so than Islam. Both Christianity and Islam represent "sister" religions that have been and continue to be by their nature dynamic, flexible, interpretive, able to accomodate varying national cultures and, finally, meaningful for all times and places. The proliferation of sects and heresies that they have spawned, at one time or another, attests to these factors and to their vitality. Perhaps the main difference between Islamic society and Western society, and their presently unequal status, results from the attitudes of the clergies and the fundamentalists in both cultures. In order to trace the evolution of clerical positions we shall regress to the time of the Crusades when Christian West met Moslem East in an atmosphere of conflict and conflagration.

To a great extent, the Crusades were a continuation of the political reconquest of Europe from Moslem rule as well as an economic venture and a social experiment, but it was religion that acted as the cement and propaganda for those wars.[2] The ultimate victory went to the Moslems and, thus, western Christianity withdrew from the lands of Islam until the nineteenth and twentieth centuries.

The Western World, for centuries after the Crusades, was absorbed by its humanistic Renaissance and its intellectual Enlightenment which permanently altered man's thinking in the West thereby ushering in modern societies. In time, the propaganda of the Crusades was forgotten in Europe and the period continues to be regarded as a romantic adventure of the Middle Ages. As part of western society, its clergy eventually came to an accomodation with the aspirations of the Enlightenment, with life in a largely secular world, and with the findings of the modern physical and social sciences. Perhaps for a few conservatives in the western churches, the question of faith and reason may still arouse feelings of discomfort. But they too have seen the validity of findings based upon scientific methodology and must accept the concepts of the social sciences, even if their aquiescence occurs with reservations.

The secular states, however, did not break completely with religious thought, for modern political science has increasingly addressed itself to many of the areas of human concern that were once dominated by the clergy. In short, Christian Socialist and Social Democratic parties encompassed the church's struggle for human justice as part of their political platforms, in Europe.[3] Thus, the modern secular state incorporated and advanced the idea of justice freeing its citizens from clerical prejudices allowing man to establish his individual relationship to God without fear of Earthly punishment by an intolerant, fanatical, religious leadership.

As secular education progressed in the United States and Europe, it enabled scholars to approach Islam free from past hostilities, prejudices or misconceptions. Academic freedom empowered scholars to present Islam and its civilization to the educated West in an extremely positive light. Since World War II, a constant review of texts and materials on Islam and the Middle East have eliminated errors of fact and opinion that survived Medieval times.[4] More recently, the Christian clergy led by the Roman Catholic Church and in conjunction with the World Council of Churches have followed the dictates of Vatican II in seeking a dialogue with moderate Moslem clergymjen in order to recast their relationship into an atmosphere of cordiality.[5] Of even greater significance for Islam in the West has been the establishment of Mosques, schools and cultural centers for Moslems living in Europe and the United States. In Belgium a special act of Parliament (July, 1974) recognized Islamic law alongside secular law[6] as valid in Europe for the first time in centuries.

These developments are seen by the Moslem fundamentalists as a result of weaknesses in the "Godless" secular world rather than expressions of freedom and equality of religion derived from humanitarian concerns which, unfortunately, are still lacking in some of the lands of Islam. Furthermore, the fundamentalists, whether lay or religious, still divide the world into two great spheres, Moslem (Dar al-Islam/the abode of Islam) and the non-Moslem (Dar al-Harb/the abode of war).   The non-Moslem West, consquently, remains in the Classical image of Crusading times - the enemy of Islam. Yet, few Moslem intellectuals have acquiesced to that point of view.

When the Western powers rediscovered the Moslem world in the nineteenth and twentieth centuries, only a few Christian fundamentalists thought of converting the Moslems to Christianity. Shortly after they arrived, they realized that preaching the Gospels to Moslems was a waste of time. Failing to win converts from Islam, those Christian missionaries reoriented their activities towards the indigenous Christian communities of the Middle East in an attempt to win them from their local churches, resulting in a shameful competition for the minds and souls of men.[7] The only truly beneficial aspect of those missionary activities resulted from the establishment of modern educational facilities opened to both Christians and Moslems. Their efforts were rewarded when the graduates of those institutions influenced others with their knowledge of modern physical and social sciences.[8] Intellectual giants committed to changing their societies soon appeared in the Middle East. Among the most prominent men in that movement were Qasim Amin, Muhammad Abdu, Mohammad Rashid Rida, Tawfiq al-Hakim, Taha Husayn and a host of Christian and Moslem Lebanese scholars from the American University of Beirut and Saint Joseph University.[9] Later graduates, classified as Christian westernizers and Moslem secularists, saw the Middle East as part of the Western world by virtue of race, religion, and intellectual heritage,[10] thus rejecting the fundamentalist world view as artificial and contrived preventing the advancement of the region and only serving to increase clerical power.

The fundamentalists, of course, held a different view of Western education and were soon to clash with the liberal intellectuals who studied in modern institutions of learning at home and abroad. But, the conservative clergy only allowed their youth to study science in the West, reluctantly. The social sciences were, however, to be studied only to understand their "enemy" better, certainly not for application at home. The fundamentalists show little interest in the study of other cultures or values for they believe that those cultures and ideas are eventually to be replaced by an Islamic way of life[11] and, hence, a hostile relationship between the two worlds, the Moslem and the non-Moslem, should endure.[12]

In defense of their beliefs, the fundamentalists of Islam point out that modern theories are the product of man's innovations and interpretations which could result in the fragmentation of Islamic doctrines and, possibly, promote new views not based upon the Islamic sciences. They follow the lead of two of the champions of Islamic fundamentalism, Taki al-Din ibn Taymiya (d. 1328) and Abd Allah al-Baydawi (d. 1388)[13] who took a literal view of the Quran, sought a return to the customs of the Prophet, and rejected all deviations (bid'ah) of opinion that were based upon rational philosophy and theology. They also interpreted the Quran and the Islamic sciences in a manner making them incompatable with Christology and the Gospels, particularly the evidence for the divinity of Jesus, but even al-Baydawi was non-commital on the clear verses in the Gospel regarding the crucifixion of Jesus.[14] Yet, the present emphasis on fundamentalism has not prevented some Islamic reformers from plunging ahead with movements aimed at social change.

The pace of social change in the Arab and Moslem world has progressed slowly but surely since the post war period, generally under the supervision of military leaders who had come to power,[15] rather than by professional politicians or a wide based intellectual enlightenment resulting in mass movements for reform. The military leaders who had championed national independence were usually replaced by a collective leadership who relyed on the newly formed but small middle class. The cultural changes they initiate from above, in the form of constitutional reforms, progresses slowly not to offend the traditionalists, conservatives or the clergy. For the Sunnite Moslems adherence to the new legislation is often restlessly accepted, but not for the Shi'ite Moslems, particularly the Iranian clergy.

In Iran, the process of modernization advances much more leisurely since the clergy, the Ayatollahs, and Khomeini in particular, regard the government as illegitmate, a userper of their authority, in accordance with Shi'ite theology. Khomeini sought exile and the liberty of France in order to conduct his campaign against the Shah and to impose his system on the citizens of Iran. Apparently, the Shah saw the Imam's departure as a concession and proceeded with a reform program known as the "White Revolution" conducted from the throne.[16]

The Shah's twelve-point program was designed to touch all segments of society and seems to have been a sincere effort to move Iran into the modern world, but inefficiency, corruption and mismanagement took its toll on the plan. The Iranian leader tried, in a limited way, to "clean up" the program in the face of growing opposition at home and abroad and, increasing pressure from the United States; but the Shah's greatest failure was his inability to sell the reform program to the masses. The overwhelming majority of the population, even when literate or semi-literate,[17] was absorbed in non-western traditional learning. Thus, only a small middle class had access to modern education and supported the Shah's reforms but they also rejected his techniques to end opposition to his regime. Perhaps most importantly, the Shah failed to explicitly tie his program of modernization to Islam. He constantly referred to the greatness of pre-Islamic Persia and spoke freely of making Iran "the Japan of the Middle East." Clearly, those phrases could not sit well with the clergy for they praised infidel societies. Furthermore, the Marxists in Iran used any opposition to the Shah as an excellent opporutnity for a campaign against his pro-western politics; but they had the foresight to claim to be Islamic Marxists in order to win some support from the masses. The Shah repressed them yet they were the only group who could have supported social modernization in his domain. (Obviously, the Shah understood his precarious position and should have guised his reforms in terms of Islamic socialism, to placate some of the clergy, as the Sunnite Moslem modernists have done.) The Shah, consequently, lost the psychological initiative to the Khomeini clique.

As the Imperial Shah continually lost ground to the clergy, the Imam encouraged the population to see the American and European presence in Iran as harmful to them.[18] All problems and misconduct were blamed on the Christian foreigners who were "running the state" through "their" Shah. The foreign community was depicted as immoral and as exploiters of Iran's wealth, while possessing nothing of value in return. The treatment of foreign women as equals by their countrymen was seen as insulting to Islam and mobs were organized to insult and berate those women in public. And, lastly, President Carter's human rights campaign regarding minorities was characterized by the Ayatollahs as interference with Islamic law and in the internal affairs of Iran. The claim of superior technology and life style in the West was viewed by the Iranian clergy as a denial of the eternal supremacy of Shi'ite Islam over all cultures and, specifically, for Ayatollah Khomeini as a transgression against his will and, perhaps more importantly, against the Word of God.

§ § §

NOTES

1. All religions are composed of three basic elements, faith, practice (rituals), and a way of life (a culture) for their adhearants. In addition, Judaism, Christianity and Islam share a common source of revelation

which guides its followers throughout their lives. See: Smith, *op. cit.*, p. 15, 17.

2. For a brief account of the political and economic aspects of the Crusades see: Richard A. Newhall, *The Crusades*, rev. ed., New York: Holt, Rinehart and Winston, Inc., 1955.

3. The founder of the Christian Socialist movement was a Catholic priest, Fr. Robert de Lamennais (1782-1854), who sought to advance social reform and justice through a Christian revival. From France, the movement spread to England and, later, it affected Protestant intellectuals. In 1891. Pope Leo XIII in his *Rerum Novarum* ("concerning new things") supported Christian socialism and democracy while attaching their ideas to liberal economic views.

4. The Middle East Studies Association of North America has reviewed teaching materials on Islam and the Middle East to improve standards of scholarship and instruction in American schools. They published their results in 1975.

5. In Febrary of 1976, the Vatican and the Libyan Arab Republic held a seminar on Moslem-Christian relations. The results of the seminar were published under the title, *Islamic Christian Dialogue*.

6. The documents of Vatican II summarized the position of the Christian churches in regard to Islam in its declaration on *The Relationship of The Church to Non-Christians* stating that "Upon the Muslim, too, the church looks with esteem...although in the course of centuries many quarrels and hostilities have arisen between Christians and Muslims, this most sacred Synod urges all to forget the past and strive sincerely for mutual understanding." Since then, the Christian churches have worked with the Islamic Council of Europe, which oversees the Moslem community in the West, to assist it in the establishment of Mosques and schools for the maintenance of Islam's heritage in the modern world. However, in recent times, differences have arisen in legal cases where Islamic law and secular law hold diverging views of justice and punishment.

    The fundamentalists of Islam caution Moslems in the West not to take European or American citizenship or alliegence seriously or faithfully for they are citizens of Allah's community whose "constitution" is the Quran. Wherever possible, they should try to gain the implementation of Islamic law alongside secular law, and to live as part of an Islamic community in the West. Economic intercourse is encouraged but social and political relations should be minimized. Thus, the Moslems are to live in the secular West but not become assimilated to it or an integral part of it, unless they can effect a transformation of those states into Moslem states.

At the current time, most of the Moslem clergy (Imams) in North America are foreign born and they are educated along the fundamentalist point of view. Their main focus in the United States is to prevent acculturation. The Islamic Coordinating Council of North America and The Federation of Islamic Associations maintains that no "American" Islam, stressing liberal American values, is possible, for Islam is "universal" with fixed values. If an American educated Moslem clergy should emerge, however, acculturation is probable.

7. It should be noted that there are no clergymen from the Eastern Christian churches seeking to undermine Christian churches in the West. And, charges of corruption aimed at those Eastern Churches by some missionaries remains unsubstantiated. The result of that competition between Christians made all of them look suspicious to their Moslem neighbors.

8. On the origins of those institutions see: P. K. Hitti, "The Impact of The West on Syria and Lebanon in The Nineteenth Century," in *Cahiers d'Histoire Mondiale*, II, 1955, pp. 608-633; Peter Avery, *Modern Iran*, New York: Frederick A. Praeger, 1967, pp. 82, 117-118; A. J. Abraham, *The Awakening of Persia: A Reconstruction of The Reign of Nasr al-Din Shah, 1848-1896*, MI.: Vande Vere Pub., Ltd., 1992.

9. For those men, Islam did not conflict with modern world values and institutions. For more on them see: Goode, *op. cit.*, p. 32; Albert Hourani, *Arabic Thought in The Liberal Age, 1798-1939*, London: Oxford University Press, 1970, pp. 130-160, 164-170, 222-224, 324-340; Von Grunebaum, *Modern Islam*, pp. 200-201, 279, 312-320.

10. The Christian westernizers and Moslem secularists held siimilar views but for different reasons. The Christians hoped that secularism would

enhance their position in the Moslem states while the Moslems wanted to rid themselves of the interference of the clergy who views hampered progress. Both groups sincerely sought to move their nations into the twentieth century. Hourani, *op. cit.*, pp. 245-259; Hisham Sharabi, *Arab Intellectuals and the West: The Formative Years, 1875-1914*, Baltimore: The Johns Hopkins Press, 1970, pp. 7-10, 66-140.

11. Von Grunebaum, *Modern Islam*, pp. 55, 57, 311; Smith, *op. cit.*, p. 92; Watt, *Islam and the Integration of Society*, p. 272.

12. Some schools of law recognize a third division, Dar al-Sulh (Dar al-Ahd) which is not under Moslem rule or law but which is a tributary of Islam by agreement. (Its significance for modern times comes from its proximity to an international treaty and for Moslems living in the West.)

13. On al-Baydawi and Ibn Taymiya see: the *Shorter I. I.*, pp. 58, 151-152.

14. Watt, *Islam and the Integration of Society*, p. 264.

15. Goode, *op. cit.*, p. 112.

16. For a brief account of the twelve point program envisioned in the "White Revolution" see: Gerard Villiers, et. al., *The Imperial Shah*, Boston: Little, Brown and Co., 1976, pp. 287-305. Amin Saikal, *The Rise and Fall of the Shah*, Princeton: Princeton University Press, 1980, pp. 71-96.

17. Illiteracy is one of the major problems facing the Moslem World. Under the Shah illiteracy was reduced but what is of greater significance is the nature of the materials one reads. The study of western science and technology is insufficient to modernize a nation. And, certainly, the ability to read traditional literature only reinforces traditional ideas and values, hence, no real progress transpires.

18. Smith, *op. cit.*, pp. 48, 86. Apparently something has gone wrong in the order of things so that the western infidel is in a position of power over the Moslems. The Moslems, possessing God's final revelation for a perfect society, are superior to all others regardless of the status of their community, a fact that will be born out in paradise, if not on Earth. Thus, the mere presence of so large a number of Americans and

Europeans in Iran assisting in the development and modernization of that state was seen by its clergy as either an admission of Islam's failure to maintain its superiority or, the preferred Moslem explanation, a new form of colonialism, or possibly both. The foreigners were seen as ruling Iran through "their" Shah while their presence and attitudes were observed as an affront to the dignity of the Khomeini faction.

CONCLUSION

Which way Islamic society will progress under fundamentalist rule can not be ascertained at this time. We have seen, however, that the Islamic sciences produced a vital force in Europe, influencing western thought in the areas of democracy, socialism and law. That interaction contributed to the creation of modern states.

Today that heritage is being strongly and effectively challenged by Moslem fundamentalists whose views tend to conflict with the cultural evolution of modern societies. Clearly, the fundamentalists are on the upswing seeking to create "Revolutions in Reverse."[1] In many ways, their activities could be compared with John Calvin's administration in Besel, Switzerland, in 1536, but, perhaps, less democratic. As in Calvin's time, the current trend in Islam may not last forever because the clergy continues to face some opposition within their states. Perhaps they have miscalculated in attempting to implement a literal interpretation of Islam and totally missed the spirit of Islam which is truly viable and innovative.

It is clear that there is much room and need for secular and religious ideas and institutions in the Moslem world and, in fact, the secular and the clerical traditions should compliment one another to enhance the evolution of human rights in Islam. And, it is hoped that as the Moslem world approaches the secular world, Moslem-Christian relations will converge in a spirit of hope, sincerity, and understanding that will surpass the cordiality of the present.

§ § §

NOTES

1. Antoine J. Abraham and Ahmed Abdul Majid, "Examining Third World Strategies," in *Contemporary Review*, vol. 241, no. 1400, p. 115.

BIBLIOGRAPHY

Primary Sources

Al-Qathafi, Muammar, *The Green Book*, part 1, *The Solution of the Problem of Democracy*, "The Authority of The People;" part 2, *The Solution of the Economic Problem*, "Socialism;" and part 3, *The Social Basis of The Third Universal Theory*, Tripoli, Lybia.

Khomeyni, Ayatollah Ruhollah, "Islamic Government," Translations on Near East and North Africa, no. 1897, *JPRS*, 72663, January, 1979.

Khoumeini, Imam, *Islam and Revolution: Writings and Declarations of Imam Khoumeini*, (trans. By Hamid Algar), Berkeley: Mizan Press, 1981.

Secondary Sources

Abraham, A. J., "The Theory and Practice of Islamic Fundamentalism," *Transnational Perspectives*, vol. 11, no. 4, 1985, pp. 20-21.

Abraham, A. J., *The Lebanon War*, Connecticut: Praeger, 1996.

Abraham, A. J., *The Awakening of Persia, The Reign of Nasr al-Din Shah, 1848-1896*, MI.: Vande Vere Publishers, Ltd., 1992.

Abraham, A. J. and Ahmed Abdul Majid, "Examining Third World Strategies," *Contemporary Review*, vol. 241, no. 1400, Sept., 1982.

Abrahamian, Ervand, *Iran: Between Two Revolutions*, New Jersey: Princeton University Press, 1982.

Avery, Peter, *Modern Iran*, New York: Frederick A. Praeger, 1967.

Burns, Robert I., S. J., Christian Islamic Confrontation in the West: The Thirteenth Century Dream of Conversion," *The American Historical Review*, vol. 76, no. 2, Dec. 1971, pp. 1386-1434.

Coulson, Noel J., *Conflicts and Tensions in Islamic Jurisprudence*, Chicago: The University of Chicago Press, 1969.

Daniel, Norman, *The Arabs and Mediaeval Europe*, London: Longman Group, Ltd., 1975.

Gaudefroy-Demombynes, Maurice, *Muslim Institutions*, (trans. By John P. Macgregor), London: Bradford and Dickens, 1950.

Gibb, H. A. R. and Harold Bowen, *Islamic Society and the West*, 2 vol., London: Oxford University Press, 1957.

Goode, Stephen, *The Prophet and the Revolutionary*, New York: Franklin Watts, Inc., 1975.

Guignebert, Charles, *The Early History of Christianity*, New York: Twayne Pub., 1927.

Halliday, Fred, *Iran: Dictatorship and Development*, New York: Penguin Books, 1980.

Hitti, P. K., "The Impact of The West on Syria and Lebanon in the Nineteenth Century," *Cahiers D'Histoire Mondiale*, II, 1955, pp. 608-633.

Hitti, P. K., *History of the Arabs*, 10th. Ed., New York: St. Martin's Press, 1970.

Hourani, Albert, *Arabic Thought in the Liberal Age, 1798-1939*, London: Oxford University Press, 1970.

Julien, Charles-Andre, *History of North Africa*, New York: Praeger, 1970.

Khadduri, Majid, *Islamic Jurisprudence, Shafi'is Resala*, Baltimore: The Johns Hopkins Press, 1961.

Khadduri, Majid and Herbert J. Liebesny, *Law in the Middle East*, vol. 1, Washington: The Middle East Institute, 1955.

Levy, Reuben, *The Social Structure of Islam*, London: Cambridge University Press, 1969.

Martin, Malachi, *The Encounter*, New York: Farrar, Straus and Giroux, 1969.

Newhall, Richard A., *The Crusades*, rev. ed., New York: Holt, Rinehart and Winston, Inc., 1955.

Nicholson, Reynold A., *A Literary History of the Arabs*, Cambridge: The University Press, 1969.

Peters, F. E., *Allah's Commonwealth*, New York: Simon and Schuster, 1973.

Qadri, Anwar Ahmed, *Islamic Jurisprudence in the Modern World*, Lahore: Ashraf Pub. House, 1981.

Ramazani, R. K., *Revolutionary Iran: Challenge and Response in the Middle East*, London: The Johns Hopkins Press, 1986.

Rizvi, Saiyid Athar Abbas, *Iran: Royalty, Religion and Revolution*, Australia: Ma'rifat Pub. House, 1980.

Rubin, Barry, *Paved with Good Intensions: The American Experience and Iran*, New York: Penguin Books, 1980.

Said, Abdul Moghny, *Arab Socialism*, Great Britain: Blanford Press, Ltd., 1972.

Saikal, Amin, *The Rise and Fall of the Shah*, Princeton: Princeton University Press, 1980.

Schacht, Joseph, *The Origins of Islamic Jurisprudence*, London: Oxford University Press, 1959.

Sharabi, Hisham, *Arab Intellectuals and the West: The Formative Years 1875-1914*, Baltimore: The Johns Hopkins Press, 1970.

Smith, Wilfred C., *Islam in Modern History*, New York: The New American Library, 1957.

Tibi, Bassam, *The Challenge of Fundamentalism, Political Islam and the New World Disorder*, Berkeley: University of California Press, 1998.

Tremlett, George, *Gadaffi, The Desert Mystic*, New York: Carroll & Graf Pub., Inc., 1993.

Villiers Gérard, et. al., *The Imperial Shah*, Boston: Little, Brown and Co., 1976.

Von Grunebaum, G. E., *Medieval Islam*, Chicago: University of Chicago Press, 1953.

Von Grunebaum, G. E., *Modern Islam*, New York: Alfred A. Knopf, 1964.

Watt, W. Montgomery, *Islam and the Integration of Society*, Great Britain: Northwestern University Press, 1961.

Watt, W. Montgomery, *A History of Islamic Spain*, Edinburgh at The University Press, 1965.

ABOUT THE AUTHOR

A. J. Abraham received his B.A. and M.A. degrees from Hunter College (CUNY) and his Ph.D. in Near and Middle Eastern History from New York University. He teaches at John Jay College (CUNY) and at New York Institute of Technology. Dr. Abraham has served as a consultant to several international agencies and organizations. A world class scholar, Professor Abraham has published over twenty articles and seven books - his latest book is entitled: *THE LEBANON WAR* (1996).